Andrew Mckie, Barrister at Clerksroom Manchester, is a specialist in claimant and defendant personal injury, with a particular interest in cases involving alleged fraud, credit hire, highways, occupiers and travel cases. Andrew is also a Director of BSB Entity Barrister-Direct which specialises in all areas of personal injury.

A Practical Guide to the 2018 Jackson Personal Injury and Costs Reforms

A Practical Guide to the 2018 Jackson Personal Injury and Costs Reforms

Andrew Mckie,
Barrister at Law, Clerksroom (Manchester) and
Director – Barrister-Direct Limited
LLB Hons, PG DIP and
Former Solicitor Advocate,
Personal Injury, Housing Disrepair and Financial Mis-selling

Law Brief Publishing

Published 2018 by Law Brief Publishing, an imprint of Law Brief Publishing Ltd
30 The Parks
Minehead
Somerset
TA24 8BT

www.lawbriefpublishing.com

Paperback: 978-1-911035-59-6

PREFACE

The second Jackson report of July 2017 introduces the idea of further fixed costs into all areas of personal injury, as well as further tariff fees in road traffic claims, fixed costs in clinical negligence, and fixed costs in multi-track cases. These changes are likely to come into effect in October 2018/ early 2019 together with additional changes to the small claims track limits.

This book aims to be a clear but comprehensive guide to all aspects of the 2018/2019 Jackson reforms that can be utilised by practitioners on a day-to-day basis, in Claimant and Defendant practice. This book has a focus on running personal injury cases in an efficient way, post-Jackson, spotting the winners and vetting the losing claims early on. The book explains the changes in a clear and comprehensive way and explores how to overcome/mitigate the changes in practice.

I wish to thank Tim Kevan of Law Brief publishing for providing me with the opportunity to write this book and the PI Brief Update website for publishing relevant sections.

Please note this book is not designed to give legal advice, and you should always consult a qualified Solicitor/Barrister about a specific set of facts.

Andrew Mckie
February 2018

CONTENTS

CHAPTER ONE
INTRODUCTION TO THE JACKSON REPORT 2017 AND CMC REGULATION: A SUMMARY OF THE CHANGES

2018/2019 is going to be a huge year for the Personal Injury world (yet again)! Changes are aloft in all different areas of Regulation. A ban on cold calling for claims companies, the movement of claims management companies towards FCA Regulation and more fixed costs for personal injury claims. This book is designed to be a comprehensive guide to take practitioners through all the changes in a clear and easily digestible way. The book will look at ways forward for Lawyers/CMCs and examine the possible outcome of the changes. This year has already seen a number of claimant law firms and CMCs go into administration, and this book seeks to offer some clear guidance as to how to look at the changes and how they may impact day-to-day practice.

Financial Guidance and Claims Bill

This piece of legislation is making its way through Parliament at the time of writing. The principle piece of legislation in terms of CMCs is a ban on cold calling and move to FCA Regulation of CMCs. It sets out as follows:-

> *To make provision establishing a new financial guidance body (including provision about cold-calling and a debt respite scheme); to make provision about the funding of debt advice in Scotland, Wales and Northern Ireland; and to make provision about regulation of claims management services*
> – https://services.parliament.uk/bills/2017-19/financialguidance-andclaims.html: -

Cold Calling:-

> *35 Cold-calling*
> *In exercising its functions the single financial guidance body must have regard to the effect of cold-calling on consumer protection and must make and publish an annual assessment of any consumer detriment.*
>
> *If the single financial guidance body considers that there are products or services where a ban on cold-calling would be conducive to its functions it 40 must advise the Secretary of State to institute bans on such cold-calling and the commercial use of any data obtained by such cold-calling.*
>
> *On receipt of advice from the single financial guidance body under subsection*
>
> *(2), the Secretary of State may by regulations made by statutory instrument introduce a ban on cold-calling and the commercial use of any data obtained 45 by such cold-calling as recommended by the single financial guidance body.*
>
> *A statutory instrument containing regulations under this section may not be made unless a draft of the instrument has been laid before, and approved by a resolution of, each House of Parliament.*
>
> *For the purposes of this section "cold-calling" refers to unsolicited real-time direct approaches to members of the public carried out by whatever means, 5 digital or otherwise.*

It is arguable that a ban on cold calling will better protect the interests of consumers. Solicitors are of course banned from cold calling, but the practice continues amongst some claims companies. Unsolicited claims do not benefit anyone in the industry and the proposed ban is to be welcomed by Solicitors. However there is some controversy around the issue. Lord Keen, discussing the changes recently said that "*Good CMCs look after their customers and if the claims management companies move into this market, that can be extremely beneficial.*"

CMCs to Move to FCA Regulation

The section of the bill that deals with this is as follows:-

PART 2 - CLAIMS MANAGEMENT SERVICES

Transfer to FCA of regulation of claims management services
The Financial Services and Markets Act 2000 is amended as follows.

23 (1) Financial Guidance and Claims Bill [HL]
Part 1 — Financial Guidance

Interpretation of Part 1

In this Part— the "debt advice function" has the meaning given in section 3(5); the "devolved authorities" means—

In section 22 (regulated activities)— in subsection (1)—
(i) the words from "to engage" to the end become paragraph (a), and
(ii) at the end of that paragraph insert ", or
(b) to engage in claims management activity.", after subsection (10) insert—

*"**(10A) "Engaging in claims management activity" means entering into or offering to enter into an agreement the making or performance of which by either party constitutes a controlled claims management activity.***

(10B) An activity is a "controlled claims management activity" if —

(a) it is an activity of a specified kind,
(b) it is, or relates to, claims management services, and
***(c) it is carried on in Great Britain.**", and*
after subsection (12) insert—

"(12A) Paragraph 25 of Schedule 2 applies for the purposes of subsection (10B) with the references to section 22 in sub- paragraph (3) of that paragraph being read as references to subsection (10B)."

Financial Guidance and Claims Bill [HL] Part 2 — Claims Management Services (a) after subsection (1A) insert—

*"**(1B) An activity is also a regulated activity for the purposes of this Act if it is an activity of a specified kind which—***
(a) is carried on by way of business in Great Britain, and
***(b) is, or relates to, claims management services.**", and 5*
(b) in subsection (3) for "subsection (1) or (1A)" substitute "subsections (1) to (1B)".

(4) In section 234C (complaints to the FCA by consumer bodies)—
(a) in subsection (1), after "financial services" insert "or of a market in Great Britain for claims management services", and
(b) in subsection (5)—
(i) in paragraph (a), at the end insert "(and "market in Great Britain" is to be construed accordingly)", and
(ii) in paragraph (b), after "financial services" insert ", or of a market in Great Britain for claims management services,".

(5) In section 234I (FCA's functions under Part 4 of the Enterprise Act 2002)—
(a) in subsection (2)(b), after "services" insert "or to the provision of claims management services in Great Britain", and
(b) in subsection (6)(a), after "financial services" insert "or in Great Britain of claims management services".

(6) In section 234J(2) (FCA's functions under the Competition Act 1998), after "financial services" insert "or relate to the provision of claims management services in Great Britain".

(7) In section 234M(1) (function of keeping market under review), after "services" insert "and the market in Great Britain for claims management services".

*(8) In section 417(1) (definitions), at the appropriate place insert—
"“regulated claims management activity” means activity of a kind specified in an order under section 22(1B) (regulated activities: claims management services);”.*

(9) After section 419 insert— “419A Claims management services

(1) In this Act “claims management services” means advice or other services in relation to the making of a claim.

***(2) In subsection (1) “other services” includes—
(a) financial services or assistance,
(b) legal representation,
(c) referring or introducing one person to another, and
(d) making inquiries,
but giving, or preparing to give, evidence (whether or not expert evidence) is not, by itself, a claims management service.***

***(3) In this section “claim” means a claim for compensation, restitution, repayment or any other remedy or relief in respect of loss or damage or in respect of an obligation, whether the claim is made or could be made—
(a) by way of legal proceedings”.***

CMCS FCA Regulation – what will this mean in practice?

1. The FCA is a much tougher regulator than the MOJ. Baroness Buscombe, sponsor of the Bill, said that "*it enables the transfer of CMC regulation by switching on FCA's regulatory, supervisory and enforcement powers in respect of claims management services, so that the FCA can design and implement a robust regulatory regime.*".

2. It is likely that many CMCs will not meet the criteria for FCA Regulation, and some will drop out of the marketplace as a result. This will likely mean in turn that many more clients will approach Solicitors directly. Barrister-Direct as a BSB entity is

FCA regulated for consumer credit activities and ATE insurance and the application process is tough and robust.

3. Schedule 4 of the Bill provides details for the transfer of the complaints handling function for CMCs from the Legal Ombudsman to the Financial Ombudsman (FOS). The FOS is a strict regulator with severe, tough penalties for non-compliance.

4. Clause 17 then ensures that the FCA has the necessary powers to restrict fees which CMCs charge in order to protect consumers from disproportionate fees.

5. The bill includes legal representation and a claim is any assistance via '*legal proceedings*', which may mean that many CMCs in the road traffic arena will cease to provide assistance to consumers if they cannot obtain appropriate FCA Regulation.

6. It can be argued that for these reasons, the CMC market may not continue to expand as quickly post-RTA reforms as some commentators expect. There is likely still to be a Solicitor market in RTA claims, albeit it will require economies of scale.

The PI Claims Market – An Overview of the Changes

With the changes to the CMC market well under way, there will also be changes implemented to the Solicitor PI market. Jackson LJ said in July 2017:-

> *"In my January 2010 report, I recommended Fixed Recoverable Costs (FRC) for 'fast track' cases (claims up to £25,000 which can be tried in one day) and costs budgeting for 'multi-track' cases (bigger claims). I also said that we would need to look again at fixing costs for cases in the lower regions of the multi-track, once the reforms which I was then recommending had bedded in.*

> *Those reforms have now bedded in, although some fast track cases still do not have FRC. Therefore, it is now opportune to consider extending FRC. To that end, on 11th November 2016 the Lord Chief Justice and the Master of the Rolls commissioned me to carry out a further review, to develop proposals for extending FRC"*
>
> *https://www.judiciary.gov.uk/publications/review-of-civil-litigation-costs-supplemental-report-fixed-recoverable-costs/*

This book is going to focus on the proposed changes to the Personal Injury Solicitor Marketplace between now and 2019, including:-

1. Fixed costs in almost all fast track cases and the 'intermediate' track. The report said:-

   > *"I recommend a grid of FRC for all fast track cases, as set out in chapter 5. Above the fast track, I recommend a new 'intermediate' track for certain claims up to £100,000 which can be tried in three days or less, with no more than two expert witnesses giving oral evidence on each side. The intermediate track will have streamlined procedures and a grid of FRC".*

   The fixed costs tables and bands are set out as below:-

   > *Band 1: RTA non-personal injury, defended debt cases.*
   > *Band 2: RTA personal injury (within Protocol), holiday sickness claims.*
   > *Band 3: RTA personal injury (outside Protocol), ELA, PL, tracked possession claims, housing disrepair, other money claims.*
   > *Band 4: ELD claims (other than NIHL), any particularly complex tracked possession claims or housing disrepair claims, property disputes, professional negligence claims and other claims at the top end of the fast track.*

Matrix of FRC for fast track claims (applies to both claimant and defendant recoverable costs)

<table>
<tr><th></th><th colspan="4">Complexity Band</th></tr>
<tr><th>Stage:</th><th>1</th><th>2</th><th>3</th><th>4</th></tr>
<tr><td>Pre-issue £1,001-£5,000</td><td></td><td>£104 + 20% of damages</td><td>£988 + 17.5% of damages</td><td rowspan="3">£2,250 + 15% of damages + £440 per extra defendant</td></tr>
<tr><td>Pre-issue £5,001-£10,000</td><td></td><td>£1,144 + 15% of damages over £5,000</td><td>£1,929 + 12.5% of damages over £5,000</td></tr>
<tr><td>Pre-issue £10,001-£25,000</td><td>£500</td><td>£2,007 + 10% of damages over £10,000</td><td>£2,600 + 10% of damages over £10,000</td></tr>
<tr><td>Post-issue, pre-allocation</td><td>£1,850</td><td>£1,206 + 20% of damages</td><td>£2,735 + 20% of damages</td><td>£2,575 + 40% of damages + £660 per extra defendant</td></tr>
<tr><td>Post-allocation, pre-listing</td><td>£2,200</td><td>£1,955 + 20% of damages</td><td>£3,484 + 25% of damages</td><td>£5,525 + 40% of damages + £660 per extra defendant</td></tr>
<tr><td>Post-listing, pre-trial</td><td>£3,250</td><td>£2,761 + 20% of damages</td><td>£4,451 + 30% of damages</td><td>£6,800 + 40% of damages + £660 per extra defendant</td></tr>
<tr><td>Trial advocacy fee</td><td>a. £500
b. £710
c. £1,070
d. £1,705</td><td>a. £500
b. £710
c. £1,070
d. £1,705</td><td>a. £500
b. £710
c. £1,070
d. £1,705</td><td>a. £1,380
b. £1,380
c. £1,800
d. £2,500</td></tr>
</table>

2. Clinical Negligence Fixed costs. The report said:-

"Clinical negligence claims are often of low financial value, but of huge concern to the individuals on both sides. The complexity of such cases means that they are usually unsuited to either the fast track or my proposed intermediate track. ***In chapter 8, I recommend that the Department of Health and the Civil Justice Council should set up a working party with both claimant and defendant representatives to develop a bespoke process for handling clinical negligence claims up to £25,000. That bespoke process should have a grid of FRC attached.*** *This scheme will capture most clinical negligence claims. Previous experience (for example, with noise induced hearing loss claims) shows that it is possible for the 'industry' to come together and develop such schemes. There is sufficient good will on both sides to achieve that in the field of clinical negligence. I remain willing to arbitrate informally on any points of disagreement.*

3. Increases to the Small Claims Track and a Ban on Pre-Medical Offers. The report sets out:-

"3.10 Whiplash reforms. On 23rd February 2017, the Government published part one of its responses to the consultation, "Reforming the soft tissue injury ('whiplash') claims process", which closed on 6th January 2017.15 ***This included a number of reforms, including the introduction of a tariff of fixed compensation for pain, suffering and loss of amenity for injuries with a duration of less than two years. Further reforms include a ban on settlement of claims without medical evidence, increasing the small claims limit for RTA related personal injury claims to £5,000, and increasing the small claims limit for all other types of personal injury claims to £2,000. The current limit for these types of claim is £1,000. The aim of these reforms is to disincentivise minor, exaggerated and fraudulent road traffic accident related soft-tissue claims, leading to projected overall sav-***

> ***ings to insurers of £1bn.*** *The Government included clauses on these reforms in the Prison and Court Reform Bill, before the June General Election necessitated the dissolution of Parliament. In the Queen's Speech on 21st June, the new Government stated its intention to proceed with whiplash reform by a new Civil Liability Bill?"*

4. A Tariff System for RTA Claims. The MOJ report on the PI Whiplash consultation proposes the following for RTA claims at:- https://www.gov.uk/government/uploads/system/uploads/attachment_data/file/593431/part-1-response-to-reforming-soft-tissue-injury-claims.pdf:- -

> *The Government has decided that the levels of compensation available under the new tariff will be as follows:*

Injury Duration	**2015 average payment for PSLA – uplifted to take account of JCG uplift (industry data)**	**JC guidelines**	**New tariff amounts**
0–3 months	£1,750	A few hundred pounds to £2,050	£225
4–6 months	£2,150	£2,050 to £3,630	£450
7–9 months	£2,600	£2,050 to £3,630	£765
10–12 months	£3,100	£2,050 to £3,630	£1,190
13–15 months	£3,500	£3,630 to £6,600	£1,820
16–18 months	£3,950	£3,630 to £6,600	£2,660
19–24 months	£4,500	£3,630 to £6,600	£3,725

5. Online Courts – the Jackson Supplemental report said:-

> ***Online Solutions Court. The Online Solutions Court will be a new court, separate from the County Court, intended for litigants to use without recourse to legal representation. It will have a simplified procedure and a strictly limited FRC regime.*** *It will deal with matters up to a value of £25,000 (including cases that currently fall within both the small claims track and the fast track).* ***However, fast track personal injury, clinical negligence, possession, intellectual property and housing disrepair claims will be excluded from its remit, as will any other case which is too complex for proper resolution within the Online Solutions Court. Such cases (with the exception of intellectual property cases) will remain in the Fast Track in the County Court.*** *Those remaining cases will be subject to the rules proposed in Chapter 5 above. In this way, the Online Solutions Court and the fast track will sit side by side, subjecting all claims below £25,000 to some form of fixed costs recovery.*

The Jackson report sets out:-

> ***1.2 The holy grail. The holy grail pursued by every civil justice reformer is a system in which the actual costs of each party are a modest fraction of the sum in issue, and the winner recovers those modest costs from the loser.*** *Germany comes closer to the ideal than we do, because it has a civil justice system fundamentally different from our own, with little disclosure and little oral evidence.1* ***In the context of a common law jurisdiction, however, there are limits on what can be achieved. Adversarial litigation is an inherently expensive process.***
>
> *1.3 What is achievable in the real world? The best that can be achieved is:*
>
> *(i) to modify the procedural rules with the aim of reducing the actual costs so far as possible;*
> *(ii) to restrict recoverable costs to that which is 'proportionate' as defined in the new proportionality rule;2 and*
> *(iii) to control the recoverable costs in advance.*

What does this all mean the in real world for PI Lawyers?

1. Costs will be fixed in most cases and more cases will be pushed into the small claims track.

2. Fixed costs will be extended into the multi track / new intermediate track.

3. RTA claims are now sought to be restricted without the help from a Lawyer.

4. We will likely see an expansion of the online Courts.

5. The Jackson report will seek to simplify some of the rules (as set out in later Chapters).

These are uncertain times for personal injury lawyers. It is clear that for the moment EL/PL/ housing and more complex PI claims will still be costs bearing. PI Lawyers must diversify in this new marketplace beyond RTA claims. An RTA claims market will only work for large volumes of claims, but EL / PL / housing disrepair and more complex PI claims will remain profitable for the foreseeable future. How long it will be before further changes will be placed upon the PI market beyond these changes remains to be seen. For the time being, PI and Clinical Negligence lawyers have plenty to be getting on with.

CHAPTER TWO
CHANGES TO STANDARD COSTS AND THE NEW INTERMEDIATE TRACK

Proportionality has been a major buzzword in the costs industry throughout 2017/2018. From April 2013, the CPR proportionality test sets out:-

44.3 Basis of assessment

(1) Where the court is to assess the amount of costs (whether by summary or detailed assessment) it will assess those costs –

(a) on the standard basis; or
(b) on the indemnity basis,
but the court will not in either case allow costs which have been unreasonably incurred or are unreasonable in amount.

(Rule 44.5 sets out how the court decides the amount of costs payable under a contract.)

(2) Where the amount of costs is to be assessed on the standard basis, the court will –
(a) only allow costs which are proportionate to the matters in issue. Costs which are disproportionate in amount may be disallowed or reduced even if they were reasonably or necessarily incurred; and
(b) resolve any doubt which it may have as to whether costs were reasonably and proportionately incurred or were reasonable and proportionate in amount in favour of the paying party.

(Factors which the court may take into account are set out in rule 44.4.)

(3) Where the amount of costs is to be assessed on the indemnity basis, the court will resolve any doubt which it may have as to whether costs

were reasonably incurred or were reasonable in amount in favour of the receiving party.

(4) Where –
(a) the court makes an order about costs without indicating the basis on which the costs are to be assessed; or
(b) the court makes an order for costs to be assessed on a basis other than the standard basis or the indemnity basis,
the costs will be assessed on the standard basis.

(5) Costs incurred are proportionate if they bear a reasonable relationship to –
(a) the sums in issue in the proceedings;
(b) the value of any non-monetary relief in issue in the proceedings;
(c) the complexity of the litigation;
(d) any additional work generated by the conduct of the paying party; and
(e) any wider factors involved in the proceedings, such as reputation or public importance.
(6) Where the amount of a solicitor's remuneration in respect of non-contentious business is regulated by any general orders made under the Solicitors Act 1974[4]*, the amount of the costs to be allowed in respect of any such business which falls to be assessed by the court will be decided in accordance with those general orders rather than this rule and rule 44.4.*

(7) Paragraphs (2)(a) and (5) do not apply in relation to –
(a) cases commenced before 1st April 2013; or
(b) costs incurred in respect of work done before 1st April 2013,
and in relation to such cases or costs, rule 44.4.(2)(a) as it was in force immediately before 1st April 2013 will apply instead.

44.4 Factors to be taken into account in deciding the amount of costs

(1) The court will have regard to all the circumstances in deciding whether costs were –

(a) if it is assessing costs on the standard basis –
(i) proportionately and reasonably incurred; or
(ii) proportionate and reasonable in amount, or
(b) if it is assessing costs on the indemnity basis –
(i) unreasonably incurred; or
(ii) unreasonable in amount.

(2) In particular, the court will give effect to any orders which have already been made.

(3) The court will also have regard to –
(a) the conduct of all the parties, including in particular –
(i) conduct before, as well as during, the proceedings; and
(ii) the efforts made, if any, before and during the proceedings in order to try to resolve the dispute;
(b) the amount or value of any money or property involved;
(c) the importance of the matter to all the parties;
(d) the particular complexity of the matter or the difficulty or novelty of the questions raised;
(e) the skill, effort, specialised knowledge and responsibility involved;
(f) the time spent on the case;
(g) the place where and the circumstances in which work or any part of it was done; and
(h) the receiving party's last approved or agreed budget.

(Rule 35.4(4) gives the court power to limit the amount that a party may recover with regard to the fees and expenses of an expert.)

The court will therefore take into account proportionality in all costs awards and assessments, unless costs are assessed on the indemnity basis. This was considered in detail (1) BRIAN MAY (2) ANITA MAY v (1) WAVELL GROUP LTD (2) FARID BIZZARI (2017), where a costs judge had misinterpreted and misapplied the test of proportionality under CPR 44.3 when carrying out a detailed assessment of costs following the claimants' early acceptance of a Part 36 offer which was significantly less than the costs sought. The rules required a costs judge, when assessing costs on the standard basis, to apply a test of reasonableness when undertaking an item-by-item assessment, before considering whether the total figure was proportionate. The Court said:-

43. *Under the previous rules the leading case on the approach to proportionality was the decision of the Court of Appeal in Lownds v Home Office [2002] 1 WLR 2450, the judgment of the court having been given by Lord Woolf MR. The Court of Appeal there held that there should be a two stage approach to assessment of costs on the standard basis (para 31), a global approach and an item by item approach. Lord Woolf held that first the court should consider whether the total sum claimed by way of costs was proportionate before turning to the individual items and determining whether they were reasonably incurred and reasonable in amount. The proportionality of the total sum was to be considered before an item by item assessment, not after. If the judge came to the conclusion that the total sum was disproportionate then he had to determine on an item by item basis whether the cost had been necessary and, if so, reasonable.* ***This gave rise, by a side wind, to a test of necessity; if costs were necessary (and reasonable) they would be proportionate****. After that item by item consideration there could be no second look at the total figure to see whether it was proportionate. The Court of Appeal were of the view that a second look at the issue of proportionality would create a "double jeopardy". The main effect of Lownds has now been explicitly reversed by the inclusion of the new final words in CPR 44.3(2)(a).*

44. *At the hearing our attention was also drawn to paragraph 39 of Lownds where the Court of Appeal considered the situation when a claimant recovered significantly less than he had claimed. The Court held that the costs judge should take the following approach:*

> *"39. Whether the costs incurred were proportionate should be decided having regard to what it was reasonable for the party in question to believe might be recovered. Thus:*
> *i. The proportionality of the costs incurred by the claimant should be determined having regard to the sum that it was*

reasonable for him to believe that he might recover at the time he made his claim...

"40. The rationale for this approach is that a claimant should be allowed to incur the cost necessary to pursue a reasonable claim but not allowed to recover costs increased or incurred by putting forward an exaggerated claim..."

45. ***Sir Rupert Jackson's view was that while a winning party should be compensated for his costs the burden of the paying party should not be greater than the subject matter of the litigation warranted, but that the guidance given by the Court of Appeal in Lownds as to the application of the proportionality test, which was intended to limit the burden on the paying party, was no longer satisfactory and needed reformulating. Costs which were disproportionate should not be payable even if they were reasonable and necessary.*** *He said, at paragraph 5.13:*

"5.13 In other words, I propose that in an assessment of costs on the standard basis, proportionality should prevail over reasonableness and the proportionality test should be applied on a global basis. The court should first make an assessment of reasonable costs, having regard to the individual items in the bill, the time reasonably spent on those items and the other factors listed in CPR 44.5(3). ***The court should then stand back and consider whether the total figure is proportionate.*** *If the total figure is not proportionate, the court should make an appropriate reduction..."*

The footnote (62) at that point reads:
"62. The test of proportionality does not, however, replace the requirement for the court to consider the bill on an item by item basis. The application of any reduction for proportionality should only take place when each item on the bill has been assessed individually."

46. ***In paragraph 5.15 of his report Sir Rupert proposed a definition of proportionality which has been adopted in the current CPR 44.3(5), as set out above. He anticipated that the application of the reasonableness test would "...usually result in a total sum which is 'proportionate'...However, if the process of assessment on the standard basis...results in a figure which is not 'proportionate', then the receiving party's entitlement to costs will be limited to such sum as is proportionate."***

His recommendations as to a new definition of proportionality have made their way as formulated by Sir Rupert into CPR 44.3(5). It seems to me that in construing the test one should focus on the wording of the rules rather than having regard to former jurisprudence which it was plainly the intention of the rule-makers to move away from. The rules were intended to give rise to a new start.

47. *In my judgment the new rules, accurately reflecting Sir Rupert's report in that respect, require a costs judge,* ***when assessing costs on the standard basis, to assess on an item by item basis whether the costs are reasonable having regard to, among other things, the factors listed in CPR 44.4(3), and to consider whether the total figure is proportionate having regard to the definition of that word in CPR 44.3(5).*** *The respondents in argument submitted that "double jeopardy" is an inherent part of the new rules and, subject to what I say below, I agree.*

48. *Since the coming into force of the new test there has been very limited authoritative guidance on its interpretation or application. Such that there is does not all appear to lead in the same direction.*

49. ***In Kazakhstan Kagazy Plc v Zhunus [2015] EWHC 404 Leggatt J commented on the new proportionality test in a case of hard fought litigation in which neither side showed any sense of moderation.*** *The sums at stake were many millions. The learned judge in that case was involved in assessing a sum to be paid on*

account of the costs of various applications which the claimant was to pay. His Lordship said in relation to proportionality as follows:

> *"13. In a case such as this where very large amounts of money are at stake, it may be entirely reasonable from the point of view of a party incurring costs to spare no expense that might possibly help to influence the result of the proceedings. It does not follow, however, that such expense should be regarded as reasonably or proportionately incurred or reasonable and proportionate in amount when it comes to determining what costs are recoverable from the other party.* ***What is reasonable and proportionate in that context must be judged objectively****. The touchstone is not the amount of costs which it was in a party's best interests to incur but the lowest amount which it could reasonably have been expected to spend in order to have its case conducted and presented proficiently, having regard to all the relevant circumstances. Expenditure over and above this level should be for a party's own account and not recoverable from the other party. This approach is first of all fair.* ***It is fair to distinguish between, on the one hand, costs which are reasonably attributable to the other party's conduct in bringing or contesting the proceeding or otherwise causing costs to be incurred and, on the other hand, costs which are attributable to a party's own choice about how best to advance its interests. There are also good policy reasons for drawing this distinction, which include discouraging waste and seeking to deter the escalation of costs for the overall benefit for litigants."***

50. *In Hobbs v Guy's and St Thomas' NHS Foundation Trust 2015 WL 6655223 Master O'Hare took a slightly different line. He reduced a claimant's bill substantially where a clinical negligence claim had settled before issue following an offer by the defendant to pay the sum of £3,500 and the claimant's costs. He considered and then applied the new proportionality test. In his view the test explained by Leggatt J in the Kazakhstan case had no application* ***"in cases such as this where the amount of reasonable costs will***

inevitably exceed the value of the claim." He held that the costs which he had found to be reasonable were nevertheless not proportionate having regard to the factors in CPR 44.3(5) and rather than reducing the global sum he disallowed individual items of expenditure which appeared to be "inconsistent with the true value of the claim". *He explained his reasons as follows:*

> *"35. The adjustment I made on grounds of proportionality reduced the total costs provisionally allowed to a figure below £10,000 (including VAT but excluding the cos of the provisional assessment). Whilst such an expenditure is high in respect of a claim of that value which settles pre-issue, I did not think it disproportionate in all the circumstances. I did not think it right to disallow the expenditure on medical records or expert reports. Even in modest value clinical negligence claims it is necessary to incur costs on these items. I did not allow these items of costs on grounds of necessity since that is trumped by proportionality. I allowed them having regard to the fact that clinical negligence claims have more complexity and involve more work than do other claims of similar value."*

51. *Last we were referred to a decision of the Senior Costs Judge,* ***Master Gordon-Saker, in BNM v MGN in which he considered and applied the new proportionality test****. The claim was for breach of confidence in publishing data taken from the claimant's phone, which she had lost. She sought a prohibitory injunction to restrain future publication, an order for delivery up of confidential information and damages. The claimant funded the litigation and protected herself by entering into conditional fee agreements with her lawyers and buying after the event insurance cover providing her with a limited indemnity against the defendant's costs. The claim was settled with the defendant giving undertakings and paying the sum of £20,000 in damages. The defendant also agreed to pay the claimant's costs of the claim, which were in the sum of £247,817 which included success fees under the conditional fee agreements and the premium for the after the event cover. The Senior Costs Judge undertook an item by item assessment of the*

reasonable costs and held them to be £167,389.45. He then undertook a separate assessment of the proportionality of those sums reducing each of them item by item, with the exception of court fees, by about half leading to a total of £84,855.80, just under a third of the original figure. The Senior Costs Judge, having commented that the new test of proportionality was intended to bring about a real change in the assessment of costs, worked through the factors in CPR 44.3(5), without slavishly identifying them by paragraph number. He concluded that while the sum in issue was modest and the value of the non-monetary relief not substantial the proceedings would not have been issued had there not been a claim for damages, and that although it was not a particularly complex case of its type the costs could bear a reasonable relationship to the value of the claim, despite exceeding it and despite the fact that it settled at an early stage, because the case was of importance to the claimant, it was specialist "Londoncentric" work, the allegations against the defendant were serious and the claimant, not knowing the use to which her information might be put, was justified in the circumstances in issuing the claim"

On the figures before him, and applying the reasoning which I have paraphrased, the Senior Costs Judge held as follows:

> ***"49. In those circumstances base profit costs of £46,000 and base counsel's fees of £14,000 must be disproportionate under the new test, being over 3 times the amount of agreed damages, and covering work which fell far short of trial. In my judgment costs of about one half of those figures would be proportionate."***

52. *Before one takes account of the success fees payable to counsel and solicitors under the conditional fee agreements which the claimant had entered into in that case and the amount of the ATE premium the "proportionate" costs as determined by the learned Master were approximately £33,550, against "the reasonable" base costs which he had assessed at £62,318, the damages having been agreed at £20,000.*

53. *We were aware that BNM was subject to an appeal to the Court of Appeal and might have an impact on the instant appeal, in which case we would have invited further submissions. Judgment was given by the court of appeal on 7 November ([2017] EWCA Civ 1767) and as we read the judgment it has no impact on the issues before us. Their Lordships did not comment on the new test or the Senior Costs Judge's application of it in the circumstances. The assessment has been remitted to him in light of the judgment of the Master of the Rolls as to the applicable test.*

54. *The comments of the learned Senior Costs Judge in BNM are therefore obiter but his approach to the application of the new test of proportionality (which was not the subject matter of consideration by the Court of Appeal) is one which we have had regard to.*

55. ***In my view the new rules intended a fresh start. It seems to me that one has to go back to the wording of sub-rule 44.3(5) and reach a judgment as to the amount of costs whose relationship with all the factors identified in that sub-rule is a reasonable one. Whether the relationship is reasonable is, in my view, a matter of judgment, rather than discretion, and, as I have said above, requires a costs judge to attribute weight, and sometimes no weight, to each of the factors (a) to (e). Further, it seems to me that the word proportionate is intended to have a consistent interpretation across rule 44.3(2), rule 44.3(5) and 44.4, which means that in considering proportionality the court is to have regard to all the circumstances (see CPR 44.4) which includes, but is not limited to, the further factors specified in CPR 44.4(3) even though they are not specifically referred to in CPR 44.3. There is a considerable degree of overlap but the plain intention is that there should be a holistic approach; the costs judge is intended to stand back and look at the overall picture.***

56. ***Whether the relationship between the costs and the relevant factors is reasonable requires an objective assessment and an objective balance to be undertaken in respect of them with a***

view to achieving the policy objectives of compensating the receiving party for his expenditure but not requiring the paying party to pay more than the litigation warranted. *Paragraphs 5.1 to 5.3 of Jackson and the comments of Leggatt J in the Kazakhstan case are support for those propositions. Leggatt J was dealing with a high value cases, but that was simply the factual context. His comments are of wider application and form part of the ratio of his decision.*

57. *The authorities also recognise the possibility that the costs may be proportionate even if they exceed the sums in issue if they bear a relationship to the specified factors which is reasonable (see BNM and Hobbs). The Master in the present case recognised such a possibility.*

58. ***The rules do not specifically state that the assessment has to be undertaken in two stages but they do require the costs judge to apply two tests, namely reasonableness and proportionality, and it is open to the costs judge to have an eye to both as he or she undertakes an item by item assessment having in mind a figure or range of figures which would be proportionate but it is equally open to the judge to apply the tests sequentially.*** *I suspect that in practice a costs judge will have both tests in mind when undertaking the item by item assessment but he or she will undertake a form of cross-checking when the total is ascertained to see whether it falls within the range of proportionate totals and then undertake an adjustment if it does not. I respectfully disagree with the learned Master insofar if it is right that he used his description of the new proportionality test as a blunt instrument as a reason to make a substantial reduction in the reasonable costs to bring them down to a rough and ready but proportionate amount. The rules, difficult as they may be to apply in practice, require the specific factors in CPR 44.3(5) to be focused on and a determination to be made as to whether there is a reasonable relationship between them. I doubt that the rules committee intended that a costs judge could or should bypass an item by item assessment and simply impose what he or she believed to be a proportionate global figure. In my*

judgment the tests of reasonableness and proportionality are intended to work together, each with their specified role, but with the intention of achieving what is fair having regard to the policy objectives which I have identified above"

Key Points:-

1. The Court is always required to stand back and look at whether costs are proportionate.

2. When assessing costs on the standard basis, to assess on an item by item basis whether the costs are reasonable having regard to, among other things, the factors listed in CPR 44.4(3), and to consider whether the total figure is proportionate having regard to the definition of that word in CPR 44.3(5).

3. What is reasonable and proportionate in that context must be judged objectively.

4. Whether the relationship is reasonable is a matter of judgment, rather than discretion, and requires a costs judge to attribute weight, and sometimes no weight, to each of the factors (a) to (e). Further, the word proportionate is intended to have a consistent interpretation across rule 44.3(2), rule 44.3(5) and 44.4, which means that in considering proportionality the court is to have regard to all the circumstances (see CPR 44.4) which includes, but is not limited to, the further factors specified in CPR 44.4(3) even though they are not specifically referred to in CPR 44.3. There is a considerable degree of overlap but the plain intention is that there should be a holistic approach; the costs judge is intended to stand back and look at the overall picture.

5. The rules do not specifically state that the assessment has to be undertaken in two stages but they do require the costs judge to apply two tests, namely reasonableness and proportionality, and it is open to the costs judge to have an eye to both as he or she

undertakes an item by item assessment having in mind a figure or range of figures which would be proportionate but it is equally open to the judge to apply the tests sequentially.

6. It is doubtful the rules committee intended that a costs judge could or should bypass an item by item assessment and simply impose what he or she believed to be a proportionate global figure. The tests of reasonableness and proportionality are intended to work together, each with their specified role.

The Intermediate Track: An Analysis

The background behind the new intermediate track was set out in the 2017 Jackson report, which can be found at https://www.judiciary.gov.uk/wp-content/uploads/2017/07/fixed-recoverable-costs-supplemental-report-online-2-1.pdf. It sets out as follows:-

> ***1 Should there be any fixed recoverable costs above the fast track?***
>
> *1.1 The debate about fixed recoverable costs above the fast track. There has been much debate about whether there is any scope for introducing a fixed costs regime above the fast track. A large part of the legal profession is opposed to any extension of fixed costs above the current limit of £25,000. They put forward two principal arguments:*
>
> *(i) Multi-track cases are so varied in character that they do not lend themselves to any rigid costs matrix.*
> *(ii) Costs management is now working well in the multi-track (as noted in the preceding chapter). Therefore, there is no need for fixed costs.*
>
> *1.2 Conclusion. I acknowledge the force of both these arguments. In particular, I accept that recent improvements in costs management reduce the need for fixed costs. Nevertheless, after considering the extensive written submissions and the debates at the seminars,* ***I have***

concluded that there is scope for fixing the recoverable costs of some categories of cases above the fast track.

1.3 Recent evidence shows that the cost of litigating lower value cases in the multi-track remains disproportionate to the value of such cases. Applying a fixed recoverable costs ("FRC") regime to suitable cases will reduce the overall costs of litigation, by encouraging efficient working, together with streamlining and limiting the amount of work that needs to be done. *It will also eliminate the process costs of budgeting or assessing the costs of such cases on an individual basis. Furthermore, fixing recoverable costs creates a clear, transparent and predictable costs structure, which will enable parties to take an informed decision at the outset as to whether a proposed claim is worth pursuing or defending. This will be particularly valuable for litigants of modest means, including small and medium-sized enterprises. As the Birmingham Law Society observed in their submissions:*

"Birmingham Law Society accepts that fixed fees can, in certain circumstances, bring certainty to parties considering and engaging in litigation. They can also offer transparency to members of the public looking to engage in litigation. As such Birmingham Law Society does not oppose the concept of fixed fees provided they are applied in the right circumstances/cases."

In my view it is now right to extend FRC above the fast track, but we must proceed with caution in order to protect access to justice.

1.4 How far above the fast track limit of £25,000 should any new FRC regime go? The Law Society, the Bar Council and others have argued that reform should be progressive and gradual, rather than a great leap forward. I accept that point. ***I also accept that we should not suddenly move to a universal FRC regime for all cases up to £250,000.*** *[In chapter 9 below, however, I propose a separate capped costs regime for certain mercantile, chancery and TCC cases up to £250,000.]* ***I propose that there should be an upper limit of***

£100,000 and that only cases of modest complexity should fall within the new FRC regime.

1.5 What sort of cases should go into the new FRC regime? The new FRC regime should apply to claims which are principally for monetary relief, such as damages or debt. The regime will include cases where declarations are sought largely to support claims for monetary relief. It will not be possible to evade the regime by including incidental claims for declaratory relief. In exceptional circumstances a claim for non-monetary relief may be assigned to the new FRC regime, where that is necessary to promote access to justice. For example:

(i) If individual householders are claiming an injunction to restrain private nuisance caused by a nearby industrial enterprise, they may not be able to proceed unless their adverse costs risk is limited by an FRC regime.
(ii) Individuals of modest means bringing defamation claims because of material on the Internet (a growing category of claimants) may only feel comfortable proceeding if their adverse costs risk is limited by an FRC regime.

2 How should such a regime be structured?

2.1 Into what track should the new fixed costs cases go? There are three views about how we should provide for the new raft of fixed costs cases. First, these cases could remain in the multi-track but be subject to an FRC regime instead of costs management. Secondly, we could simply expand the fast track. The third option is to create a new track, sitting between the fast track and the multi-track, to provide for such cases. After full discussion at an assessors' meeting, the first option was rejected as impracticable. FRC cases will require a different case management regime and they will not be subject to costs management. You cannot have two entirely different streams of cases in the same track. So, the choice really lies between the second and third options.

2.2 I favour the third option for three reasons:
(i) The fast track works well. Practitioners are familiar with it. I do not want to change the character of a track which works well and already caters for a large proportion of all contested cases.
(ii) Cases in the bracket £25,000 to £100,000 will usually be more complex than fast track cases. They may require more elaborate evidence and take longer to try. The procedural rules for such cases should therefore be different from those in CPR Part 28.
(iii) The fast track upper limit of £25,000 coincides with the planned upper limit of the Online Solutions Court. When that court comes into existence it will replace the fast track as the normal court for many categories of claims up to £25,000: see paragraphs 6.92-6.102 of Briggs LJ's Final Report.2 My proposed track will sit immediately above (a) the Online Solutions Court and (b) the residue of the fast track. Joined up law reform requires that the different civil justice initiatives should dovetail together, as the former President of the Law Society emphasised in his speech at the London seminar.

2.3 What should the new track be called? I propose that the new track be called the 'intermediate track'.

3 Allocation of cases to the intermediate track

3.1 Value cannot be the sole criterion. Many of the submissions make two important points. First, value must not be the sole criterion for assigning cases to an FRC regime: some high value cases are straightforward; some low value cases are complex; some cases are difficult to value. Secondly, if the recoverable costs are going to be fixed, the procedure must be streamlined, so that lawyers on both sides do less work. It follows from this second point that only cases suitable for a streamlined procedure should be allocated to the intermediate track.

3.2 Proposed criteria. I propose that the following be the criteria for allocating a case to the intermediate track:

(i) The case is not suitable for the small claims track or the fast track.

(ii) The claim is for debt, damages or other monetary relief, no higher than £100,000. [The value of the case may change during the litigation for a variety of reasons. In the ordinary way, cases should remain within the track and band to which they were originally assigned. But if the case changes fundamentally, for example because the defendant admits part of the claim, then the court should have power to re-allocate.]
(iii) If the case is managed proportionately, the trial will not last longer than three days.
(iv) There will be no more than two expert witnesses giving oral evidence for each party.
(v) The case can be justly and proportionately managed under the expedited procedure described in section 4 below.
(vi) There are no wider factors, such as reputation or public importance, which make the case inappropriate for the intermediate track.
(vii) The claim is not for mesothelioma [There is a bespoke procedure for mesothelioma claims in Practice Direction 3D] or other asbestos related lung diseases.
(viii) Alternatively, even if none of criteria (i)-(vii)are met, there are particular reasons to assign the case to the intermediate track, of the kind described in paragraphs 3.7-3.8 below.

3.3 Why exclude mesothelioma and other asbestos related lung diseases? These claims are managed in accordance with the procedure in the Mesothelioma Practice Direction (Practice Direction 3D). They are case managed in specific courts in specialist Asbestos Lists by judges experienced in this work. The law applying to the determination of such claims is in accordance with other personal injury claims, but in addition specific statutes and case law apply. The value of such claims varies. A few are of a value and/or level of complexity that would otherwise come within the intermediate track, principally claims for diffuse Pleural thickening (many of which include a claim for provisional damages). Even so, I think that they should be excluded from the FRC regime. There is not always a clear distinction between mesothelioma cases and pleural thickening cases because (i) quite frequently the diagnosis is not clear-cut, at least in the early stages, and (ii) some claimants with relatively benign conditions will go on to develop mesothelioma or lung cancer or disabling respiratory disease. The Asbestos Lists are well used, operate very efficiently and have been the subject of few complaints from either claimants or defendant insurers. It would inevitably cause inefficiencies if some of these claims were removed from the specialist management provided by Practice Direction 3D, and case managed differently from other mesothelioma claims. That would defeat the aim of the Practice Direction.

3.4 What about complex personal injury claims and professional negligence claims? The criteria in paragraph 3.2 will exclude those complex personal injury and professional negligence cases which the Personal Injuries Bar Association and the Professional Negligence Bar Association maintain are unsuitable for FRC. My hope and expectation is that the criteria in paragraph 3.2 will catch only those cases which are suitable for FRC.

3.5 What about clinical negligence cases? As discussed in chapter 8 below, there is reason to believe that a bespoke process for clinical negligence claims up to £25,000 (including claims where breach and causation are in issue) with an accompanying grid of FRC, will result from the work which is in hand. ***Clinical negligence claims above £25,000 will seldom be suitable for the intermediate track, unless both breach of duty and causation have been admitted at an early stage. The multi-track will be the normal track for clinical negligence claims above £25,000.***

3.6 Will some other categories of case generally be unsuitable for the intermediate track? Yes. On the basis of the above criteria, the intermediate track will seldom be suitable for (a) some multi-party cases; (b) actions against the police5 (as demonstrated by the submissions of the Police Action Lawyers Group); (c) child sexual abuse claims (as demonstrated by the submissions of the Association of Child Abuse Lawyers); and (d) intellectual property cases.

3.7 Additional discretion. The court should have a residual discretion to allocate any case not satisfying the criteria set out in paragraph 3.2 above (including any claim for non- monetary relief) to the intermediate track, where such allocation is necessary in order to promote access to justice. Paragraph 1.5 above gives examples of cases where such an order may be necessary to promote access to justice.

3.8 Cases where for other reasons recoverable costs should be limited. In some categories of litigation, where emotions are apt to run high, parties may need to be protected from their own enthusiasm for the fray. If mediation is unsuccessful or unacceptable to such parties, the straitjacket of the intermediate track may save them from ruinous litigation. This would be a factor to bear in mind on allocation.

3.9 The bands. ***Band 1 will be for the least complex cases in the intermediate track. A simple claim over the fast track limit, where there is only one issue and the trial will take a day or less, would generally be suitable for that band: for example, many debt claims or quantum only personal injury claims would be suitable for Band 1. Band 4 will be for the most complex cases in the intermediate track: Examples may be disputes about family businesses or boundary disputes between neighbours, where the disputed land has no great value. employers' liability disease claim where there are serious issues of fact/law and the trial is likely to last three days. Bands 2 and 3 will be the 'normal' bands for intermediate track cases, with the more straightforward cases going into Band 2 and the more complex cases going into Band 3. [For further discussion of how these principles will apply to personal injury and non-personal injury cases, see paragraphs 5.9 to 5.11 below.]***

3.10 Pre-action process. The pre-action protocols should be amended to require the parties to endeavour to agree pre-action (a) the appropriate track for cases and (b) in respect of intermediate track cases, the appropriate band. Claimants should state their proposals in this regard in the letter of claim. Defendants should do the same in the letter of response. *If the case settles before* *issue or before allocation without any agreement on the appropriate track and band, then a decision on that issue should fall to the judge assessing costs.*

3.11 Assignment to bands at the allocation stage. On allocating a case to the intermediate track, the judge will (either by agreement between the parties or by reference to the directions questionnaires) assign it to Band 1, Band 2, Band 3 or Band 4. On issue, the claimant will have ascribed a value to their claim for court fee purposes. *That may assist the judge in the task of allocating cases to tracks and bands. At the subsequent case management conference ("CMC"), either party may challenge the assigned band. If the only reason for holding a CMC is the dispute about assignment, the unsuccessful party on that issue should incur a costs liability of £300 to the successful party.*

3.12 Need for a practice direction. There will need to be a practice direction for the intermediate track. This practice direction will include specific guidance on assignment to bands. [In the same way that the current CPR rule 26.8 gives guidance on allocation to tracks.] Matters which are obviously relevant are: complexity of the factual and legal issues, volume of evidence, remedy sought and value of claim. A new directions questionnaire must be designed to elicit the information which the court will need for this task.

3.13 Exiting the intermediate track. The court must have a residual power to take cases out of the intermediate track. It may be necessary to do so if the nature of the case changes fundamentally. The discretion should be strictly limited. Otherwise litigants will not enjoy certainty as to costs, which is one of the principal benefits of the fixed costs regime. I propose that the court should only be permitted to take cases out of the intermediate track after the first CMC "in exceptional circumstances".

4 Procedure for cases in the intermediate track

4.1 Requirement for a streamlined procedure. As previously noted, many of the written submissions have stressed that if recoverable costs are to be fixed, then the work to be done by the parties or their lawyers must also be controlled. This is necessary to ensure that the litigation process is efficient, so that only those steps that "are genuinely required in order to take a case to a fair trial" are taken (submission of the City of London Law Society). The procedure I propose below is intended to achieve that objective. Obviously, any rules embodying such a procedure must contain the familiar proviso "unless the court otherwise orders".

4.2 Statements of case. ***Each statement of case shall be no longer than 10 pages [In order to avoid argument about font size, the limit could be specified as a certain number of words. The same comment applies to all the suggested page limits in this chapter.] and shall be served together with any core document [In this context "core documents" means (a) documents relied upon by the party and (b) documents which are obviously necessary for other parties to understand the case they have to meet.] which are not in the possession of other parties. It should not be possible,*** *however, to evade the intermediate track by deliberately drafting particulars of claim to exceed the specified length. The court at the CMC will simply order the claimant to re-draft the pleading more concisely and at its own expense.*

4.3 CMC. At the CMC, the court will review and approve a list of issues, resolve any disputed document requests, consider alternative dispute resolution ("ADR"), give directions and fix a date for the trial and (if it is needed) the pre-trial review ("PTR"). ***The court will also identify the specific matters to which any oral evidence should be directed and will limit the number of factual witnesses in the exercise of its powers under CPR rule 32.2 (3).*** *Although trials up to three days in length fall within the parameters of the intermediate track, both the advocates and the judge should bear in mind that trial days are the most expensive stage of the litigation and involve* *the most inconvenience to parties and witnesses (although not to lawyers, for whom trials are normal work). Therefore, they should together design case management directions to keep the trial as short as possible, ideally no more than one day.*

4.4 Disclosure in non-personal injury cases. CPR rules 31.5 (3) to (8) shall not apply. Instead, each party shall disclose:
(i) The documents upon which it relies, in so far as not previously disclosed;
(ii) Any documents or classes of documents which the court specifically orders at the CMC. The parties will exchange document requests seven days before the CMC.

4.5 Disclosure in personal injury cases. In personal injury litigation, disclosure is not generally a driver of high costs. Therefore, my Final Report recommended that personal injury litigation should be exempted from the proposed new disclosure rules: see chapter 37 paragraph 3.14. That recommendation was accepted and CPR rule 31.5 (2) exempts personal injury litigation from the new disclosure rules introduced in April 2013. For essentially the same reasons, ***I would exempt personal injury litigation from the proposed disclosure rules in the intermediate track. Standard disclosure will be the normal order in personal injury cases.***

4.6 Factual evidence. Written witness statements shall stand as evidence-in-chief. The total length of all the witness statements of a party shall not exceed 30 pages.

4.7 Expert evidence. Oral expert evidence shall be limited to one or, if reasonably required and proportionate, two expert witnesses for each party. Each expert report shall be no more than 20 pages. This limit does not apply to any necessary photographs, plans and academic or technical articles attached to the report. In appropriate cases opposing experts shall give their evidence concurrently, in accordance with section 11 of Practice Direction 35.

4.8 Trial. Oral evidence at trial shall be directed to the specific matters identified by the court at the CMC or subsequently. The court will set time limits for oral evidence and submissions (so far as it is necessary to do so), in order to complete the trial within its allotted span.

4.9 Applications. So far as possible, all applications should be made at the CMC. The rules for any applications made after the CMC should be:
(i) All applications and documents filed in support must be concise.
(ii) The respondent must answer in writing within 7 days of service of the application notice. The response must be concise.
(iii) Any reply from the applicant must be provided within two business days of service of the response and be concise.
(iv) The court will deal with an application without a hearing unless the court considers it necessary to hold a hearing. In appropriate cases that may be a hearing by telephone.
(v) The court will decide who shall pay the costs of any interim application and summarily assess them. Any such costs order will be additional to FRC.

4.10 Vexatious applications. The Bar Council make the point that the court must control "the scope and number of any interim applications or procedural gamesmanship". They give as examples repeated applications by a deep pocket party for specific disclosure or for answers to CPR Part 18 requests. I agree. The court should deal with such tactics by applying the rules governing unreasonable litigation conduct: see below.

4.11 Hand down of judgment. Whereas judges usually give ex tempore judgments in fast track cases, they will often wish to reserve judgment in intermediate track cases. This will necessitate a separate hand down hearing. It will be possible to dispense with the attendance of parties or advocates, if they have agreed all consequential matters. In the absence of such agreement, a short hearing is probably more efficient than continuing correspondence between the parties or their representatives.

5 Fixed recoverable costs

5.1 How should FRC be structured? This has been the subject of much debate, in particular at the Cardiff seminar. The Precedent H phases are suitable for costs management, but inevitably they generate argument about how much work in a particular phase has been done. Also, a party may do work earlier than is necessary for tactical reasons. In my view, the better approach for FRC is to draw up a grid by reference to chronological stages. [As one of my assessors DJ Middleton and Stephen Webber (an experienced litigation solicitor) argued at the Cardiff seminar.] This has worked in the fast track over the last four years and it brings greater certainty.

5.2 Ring fencing fees for counsel. Many practitioners, both solicitors and barristers, have urged the importance of ring fencing fees for counsel. The involvement of counsel at an early stage, both in advising and drafting, brings substantial benefits. Independent counsel bringing a fresh eye to the case can focus the litigation and sometimes bring about settlement. On the other hand, the rules cannot insist upon the use of counsel. Many other specialist lawyers bring the same benefits. In my view, for the reasons set out in chapter 5, the best course is to specify fees for items of work which are to be done by counsel or specialist lawyers.

5.3 Proposed grid. I propose a grid of FRC for intermediate track cases as set out in table 7.1 below. The grid must be read subject to the following rules:

(i) In the grid the word 'damages' is used as shorthand for damages, debt, liquidated sum or other monetary relief.
(ii) If the claimant succeeds, the specified percentage applies to the sum recovered. If the defendant succeeds, the specified percentage applies to the claim defeated, as valued in the particulars of claim.
(iii) The figures in each of stages S1, S3, S4, S5, S6 and S8 are the cumulative totals for costs incurred up to and including that stage. I have shaded these cumulative boxes for ease of use.

(iv) The figures in stages S2, S7 and S9-S15 are separate sums for those items, if carried out.
(v) The figures in stages S2, S7 and S13 are ring-fenced for counsel or a specialist lawyer. The sums in the other boxes are for division between the solicitors and counsel/specialist lawyer as appropriate in the individual case.
(vi) For non-personal injury cases which are settled before issue, the figures in stage S1 are capped costs, rather than FRC.

Table 7.1

Stage (S)	*Band 1*	*Band 2*	*Band 3*	*Band 4*
S1 Pre-issue or pre-defence investigations	*£1,400 + 3% of damages*	*£4,350 + 6% of damages*	*£5,550 + 6% of damages*	*£8,000 + 8% of damages*
S2 Counsel/ specialist lawyer drafting statements of case and/or advising (if instructed)	*£1,750*	*£1,750*	*£2,000* [12]	*£2,000* [13]
S3 Up to and including CMC	*£3,500 + 10% of damages*	*£6,650 + 12% of damages*	*£7,850 + 12% of damages*	*£11,000 + 14% of damages*
S4 Up to the end of disclosure and inspection	*£4,000 + 12% of damages*	*£8,100 + 14% of damages*	*£9,300 + 14% of damages*	*£14,200 + 16% of damages*
S5 Up to service of witness statements and expert reports	*£4,500 + 12% of damages*	*£9,500 + 16% of damages*	*£10,700 + 16% of damages*	*£17,400 + 18% of damages*
S6 Up to PTR, alternatively 14 days before trial	*£5,100 + 15% of damages*	*£12,750 + 16% of damages*	*£13,950 + 16% of damages*	*£21,050 + 18% of damages*
S7 Counsel/ specialist lawyer advising in writing or in conference (if instructed)	*£1,250*	*£1,500*	*£2,000*	*£2,500*
S8 Up to trial [14]	*£5,700 + 15% of damages*	*£15,000 + 20% of damages*	*£16,200 + 20% of damages*	*£24,700 + 22% of damages*
S9 Attendance of solicitor [15] *at trial per day* [16]	*£500*	*£750*	*£1,000*	*£1,250*

[12] *£3,000 if there is a counterclaim and defence to counterclaim. The rules may need to specify how costs are split between claim and counterclaim.*

[13] *£3,000 if there is a counterclaim and defence to counterclaim. The rules may need to specify how costs are split between claim and counterclaim.*

[14] *If the receiving party did not prepare the bundle, subtract: (a) £500 for a Band 1 case, (b) £750 for a Band 2 case, (c) £1,000 for a Band 3 case, and (d) £1,250 for a Band 4 case.*

[15] *In this table "solicitor" includes a representative of the solicitor's firm*

[16] *To be halved if attendance is for half a day or less.*

Stage (S)	*Band 1*	*Band 2*	*Band 3*	*Band 4*
S10 Advocacy fee: day 1	*£2,750*	*£3,000*	*£3,500*	*£5,000*
s11 Advocacy fee: subsequent days [17]	*£1,250*	*£1,500*	*£1,750*	*£2,500*
S12 Hand down of judgment and consequential matters	*£500*	*£500*	*£500*	*£500*
S13 ADR: counsel/specialist lawyer at mediation or JSM (if instructed)	*£1,200*	*£1,500*	*£1,750*	*£2,000*
S14 ADR: solicitor at JSM or mediation	*£1,000*	*£1,000*	*£1,000*	*£1,000*
S15 Approval of settlement for child or protected party	*£1,000*	*£1,250*	*£1,500*	*£1,750*
Total: (a) £30,000 (b) £50,000, (c) £100,000 damages [18]	*(a) £19,150 (b) £22,150 (c) £29,650*	*(a) £33,250 (b) £37,250 (c) £47,250*	*(a) £39,450 (b) £43,450 (c) £53,450*	*(a) £53,050 (b) £57,450 (c) £68,450*

[17] To be halved if attendance is for half a day or less.

[18] Assuming a one day trial in Band 1, a two day trial in Band 2, and a three day trial in Bands 3 and 4. For all bands, it is assumed that there was no counterclaim, that the receiving party prepared the trial bundles, that there was unsuccessful ADR and that there was no approval of settlement for a child or protected party.

5.4 Why should the figures in stage S1 be FRC in personal injury cases but capped costs in other cases? In personal injury cases, there is a minimum amount of work which must be done to achieve a settlement pre-issue. On a 'swings and roundabouts' basis the S1 figures can fairly stand as FRC in personal injury cases. In non-personal injury cases, the amount of work to be done to achieve a pre-issue settlement may vary substantially. In some cases, a simple letter of claim may suffice to bring about a settlement. In other cases, a large amount of investigation may be required.

5.5 How are the costs figures derived? The figures in Table 7.1 are based upon (a) Professor Fenn's analysis of data on personal injury cases received from Taylor Rose TTKW, [Solicitors and costs lawyers] (b) discussions with the assessors, (c) consideration of the budget exercise, the submissions and data received and (d) my view as to how CPR rule 44.3 (5) (defining proportionality) should be applied to cases falling within the intermediate track. By way of elaboration:

(i) The graphs at appendix 9 show all 1,461 observations extracted from the Taylor Rose TTKW dataset relating to multi-track claims settled since the coming into force of the Legal Aid, Sentencing and Punishment of Offenders Act 2012 with damages less than £100,000 and where the claimants had provided no more than three expert reports. Each separate chart in the graphs contains those observations on claims that were settled at four different chronological stages of litigation - pre-issue, pre-CMC, pre-expert exchange, pre-PTR. The dots show the observed combinations of agreed costs and damages at settlement for each claim, where agreed costs are measured on the vertical axis, and damages on the horizontal axis. Within each chart,

several lines are drawn through the data. The lines labelled "Band 1" (i.e. the first from the bottom in each chart) show the expected agreed costs as estimated for varying levels of damages for the claims categorised as non-personal injury road traffic accident ("RTA"). The lines labelled "Band 2" (i.e. the second from the bottom in each chart) show the expected agreed costs as estimated for varying levels of damages for the claims categorised as RTA, employers' liability accident, or public liability. The lines labelled "Band 3" (i.e. the third from the bottom in each chart) show the expected agreed costs as estimated for varying levels of damages for the claims categorised as employers' liability disease. The lines labelled "Band 4" represent an attempt, by extrapolation and based on judgement, to characterise the relationship between agreed costs and damages for the most complex claims, irrespective of claim type. A formula is derived to produce each of these lines for the purposes of Table 7.1. The slope of each line is used to determine the '% of damages' figure attached to Bands 1 to 3. From inspecting the graphs, it is evident that as the complexity of the case (and the stage of litigation at settlement) increases the slope becomes steeper, and this leads to a higher '% of damages' figure. Based on the formula derived for each line, the lump sums are calculated as constant amounts of costs, irrespective of the level of damages. This is the point at which each line intersects the vertical axis. The Band 4 '% of damages' and lump sums are based on judgement for the most complex cases, using a similar relationship between agreed costs and damages to the other bands. Further explanation of how these formulae were estimated can be found in appendix 9.

(ii) I have then added to the fixed costs formulae the figures in the boxes for stages 2 and 7, in order to ring fence fees for counsel or specialist lawyers, as urged by many of those who sent in submissions or who spoke at seminars. In boxes S9 – S12 I have added in trial costs. (Almost all of the cases analysed by Professor Fenn settled before trial and so did not include these costs.) Next, I have added in ADR costs. In personal injury cases below £100,000, this usually means direct negotiations or a joint settlement meeting. In non-personal injury cases below £100,000, ADR may involve a mediation. Finally, box

S15 provides for settlements which may require court approval. That is discussed further in paragraph 6.2 below.

(iii) The figures in table 7.1 are broadly in line with the data set out in chapter 3 above (as discussed in paragraph 5.7 below) and with the experience of those assessors involved in the budgeting of cases suitable for the intermediate track. [Allowance must be made for process savings (because of FRC) and efficiency savings (because of the streamlined procedure for the intermediate track).] The figures in Bands 2 and 3 are reasonably close, because (a) that is where Professor Fenn's analysis of the Taylor Rose data leads and (b) most cases in this range tend to gravitate towards the centre. Bands 1 and 4 are for those cases which are simpler or more complex respectively.

5.6 Are you being more 'generous' than a strict derivation from the Fenn graphs? Yes. First, all the costs for stages S2, S7 and S9-S15 are all additional to the costs derived from the Fenn graphs. Secondly, the Band 4 figures go above that which can be derived statistically from the data, but fit with my own and my assessors' understanding of what are reasonable costs for the most complex types of case likely to go into the intermediate track.

5.7 How do the figures in Table 7.1 compare with the data in chapter 3? In my view, there is a reasonable fit with the data in sections 2 and 4 of chapter 3, if one bears in mind the following:

(i) There will be 'process' savings, if recoverable costs are fixed.
(ii) There will be 'efficiency' savings consequent upon the streamlined procedure proposed in this chapter.
(iii) Approved budgets and many of the costs figures quoted in chapter 3 include
disbursements which are additional to the sums shown in Table 7.1.
(iv) Not all of the cases up to £100,000 in value will go into the new intermediate track – only those which meet the criteria set out in this chapter. Many of the multi-track cases reviewed in chapter 3 self-evidently do not meet those criteria.

5.8 For the above exercise, I have ignored data received concerning cases which are unlikely to go into the intermediate track, such as substantial defamation claims and actions against the police. The damages in such cases may not be high, but their complexity indicates that they will not generally be suitable for the intermediate track.

5.9 How will the four-column grid be used in personal injury cases? Straightforward cases, where only one issue (such as quantum) is in dispute, will generally go into Band 1. Cases where both liability and quantum are in dispute will generally go into Band 2 or Band 3. Cases where there are serious issues on breach, causation and quantum (but which still fall within the intermediate track) will go into Band 4.

5.10 What about non-personal injury cases? Straightforward cases, where only one issue is in dispute (e.g. proving a debt), will generally go into Band 1. Most intermediate track cases will go into Band 2 or Band 3. Complex cases falling within the intermediate track will go into Band 4. The recoverable costs set out in Table 7.1 represent my best effort at converting the proportionality rules into hard figures. This must be the correct approach. [See The Reform of Civil Litigation, published by Sweet & Maxwell in September 2016, chapters 3 and 19.] The grid cannot be an exact pre-estimate of the costs which every party will incur in every intermediate track case. We do not have, and we never will have, large volumes of evidence about the costs of different types of non-personal injury cases comparable to the material available on personal injury claims. As the Chancery Bar Association observed in their paper on fixed costs last year:

> *"Traditionally litigants have had to expect to pay a substantial shortfall in the event of success where they are awarded costs on a standard basis."*

5.11 Comparability of personal injury and non-personal injury cases. There is, I suggest, sufficient flexibility in the grid to accommodate the general run of personal injury and non- personal injury cases which fall within the intermediate track. Also, as one of my assessors has pointed out, within the intermediate track we should not be putting a higher price on property and financial claims than on claims about human health.

5.12 Disbursements. The above table does not include disbursements. The principal disbursements will be court fees, expert fees and (where ADR takes the form of mediation) the mediator's fee. In some cases, translators and/or interpreters are needed. I recommend that once the new fixed costs regime is in place, work should commence on developing fixed costs for experts. This is essentially what happened in the fast track. Once the fast track fixed costs for personal injury cases had been in place for a year, a scheme of fixed costs for medical reports [In respect of soft-tissue injury RTA claims, which represent a large proportion of fast track personal injury claims.] was introduced: see chapter 15, paragraph 5.22 of my previous report and CPR rule 45.19. It would also be sensible to develop fixed costs for mediators, translators and interpreters.

5.13 ***Defendant's failure to beat claimant's Part 36 offer. If the defendant fails to beat an effective claimant offer under CPR Part 36, for the reasons set out in chapter 5 above and subject to the same caveats, I tentatively propose that there should be a 30% or 40% uplift on costs rather than indemnity costs.***

5.14 Unreasonable litigation conduct. In cases of unreasonable litigation conduct, [see Dammermann v Lanyon Bowdler LLP [2017] EWCA Civ 269 at [30]-[32]] As to what constitutes unreasonable litigation conduct, [Either 30% or 40%, depending upon what is decided in relation to the preceding paragraph] the court should have the power either to award a percentage uplift on costs or to make an order for indemnity costs. The court will exercise that power, having regard to the seriousness of the conduct in question. One example of such unreasonable conduct might be substantial non-compliance with the relevant pre-action protocol.

5.15 London weighting. The current FRC rules in the fast track provide for a 12.5% uplift on fixed costs payable to a party who lives in the London area and instructs a legal representative who practises in the London area: see CPR rule 45.29C (2), rule 45.29F (5) and Practice Direction 45 paragraph 2.6. I recommend that similar rules should apply to the extended FRC regime proposed in this chapter.

5.16 Uprating for inflation. I recommend that FRC in the intermediate track should be adjusted for inflation every three years, in the same manner as set out in chapter 5 concerning FRC in the fast track.

5.17 Contractual entitlement to costs. Any intermediate track case where one party has a contractual entitlement to costs will be subject to the streamlined procedure set out in this chapter. If the party with a contractual entitlement to costs is successful, the position will be as set out in chapter 5, paragraph 3.7. It is not within my terms of reference to consider whether the substantive law in this area should be reformed and I do not address that question.

6 Should the intermediate track include Part 8 claims?

6.1 Not yet. Some financial claims which proceed under CPR Part 8 would be suitable for FRC, as was noted at the Leeds seminar. It would be possible to modify the grid in Table 7.1 to accommodate those claims. The assessors and I have discussed at some length whether to propose FRC for such claims in this report. In the end, we have all concluded that such a step would be premature. For the time being, the costs of such claims should, where appropriate, be controlled by costs management. It is first necessary to let the intermediate track and the proposed FRC for Part 7 claims bed in. Many of the submissions to the review call for a gradualist approach to developing FRC. In relation to this issue, I heed their call. Subject to the minor exceptions set out below, I recommend that the question of extending FRC to Part 8 claims should be deferred for future consideration.

6.2 Approval of settlements for children and protected parties. Table 7.1 includes FRC for the approval of settlements for children and protected parties. If the settlement is pre-issue, the application for approval is made under CPR Part 8. If proceedings are on foot, the application for approval is made under CPR Part 23. In any intermediate track case, the FRC for that application should be the same, regardless whether it is made under Part 8 or Part 23. [Court fees will, of course, be a recoverable disbursement.]

6.3 Costs only proceedings. Costs only proceedings are brought under CPR Part 8. The receiving party files short particulars of claim referring to the settlement agreement, the defendant files an acknowledgement of service and the court makes an order for assessment of costs. I recommend that the FRC for a claimant in such proceedings should be £300 and for a defendant in such proceedings [The paying party may occasionally secure an order for costs: for example, if the costs only proceedings fail for some reason or if there is a relevant CPR Part 36 offer.] £150.

6.4 And finally. It should be noted that Part 8 is already used, in modified fashion, for determining quantum in low value personal injury cases not settled within the Portal. These cases already have FRC. They are excluded from the general rule that Part 8 claims are allocated to the multi-track. These arrangements will continue and are unaffected by my proposals in this chapter. These figures are, of course, exclusive of court fees and VAT.

7 The future

7.1 Bedding in of these reforms and future review. If the above proposals are accepted, I recommend that after four years there be a review of these arrangements. If they are working satisfactorily, then the Civil Procedure Rule Committee ("the Rule Committee") may decide to expand the scope of the intermediate track to include:

(i) Monetary claims above £100,000;
(ii) Claims for non-monetary relief.

7.2 Such an approach would give the reforms time to bed in, as well as enabling the Rule Committee to address any issues that arise. As one major insurer put it in their submission:

> *"any revised approach to fixed costs should be, to a degree, evolutionary so as to ensure that they are fair; proportionate; facilitate access to justice; make efficient use of limited and valuable court time and resources and prevent unintended consequences".*

7.3 Analogy with the fast track. Such an approach would also replicate our experience with the fast track. There have been FRC for part of the fast track since July 2013. It is now widely accepted that it is appropriate to expand the scope of that fixed recoverable costs regime.

7.4 Developing more bespoke processes. I refer in chapter 8 to work which is in hand to develop bespoke processes for clinical negligence claims. There is scope for more work of this nature in respect of other areas of high volume litigation. Claimant and defendant representatives have worked together to develop bespoke processes for handling low value RTA claims and noise induced hearing loss claims. They have also worked together constructively to develop the Serious Injury Guide. Both the Association of Personal Injury Lawyers and the liability insurers speak warmly of that collaboration in their submissions.

Liability insurers lament that there is a gap between the fast track cases on the one hand and serious injury cases on the other, where there has been no such co-operation. They state:

> *"The parties (on both sides) have not worked together to create a consumer-friendly way of resolving disputes above the fast track threshold."*

I see much force in that comment and recommend that the collaboration between claimant bodies and liability insurers should now extend to areas of litigation above the fast track (whether or not within the intermediate track). This would be to the benefit of claimants as well as liability insurers and the legal profession. A regime of FRC can probably be developed on the back of any further bespoke processes.

8 Conclusion

8.1 Recommendations. I recommend that:

(i) A new intermediate track with a streamlined procedure should be created for cases above the fast track, which are of modest complexity and up to a value of £100,000.
(ii) There should be a grid of FRC for such cases, as set out in this chapter, and the figures should be reviewed every three years.
(iii) There should be FRC for (a) applications to approve settlements for children and protected parties and (b) costs only proceedings, in respect of intermediate track cases.
(iv) Save as set out in (iii), CPR Part 8 claims should be excluded from the proposed FRC regime.
(v) After these reforms have bedded in, consideration should be given to extending the scope of the intermediate track and the range of FRC.

Key Points:-

1. There will be no immediate move for all cases up to £250,000, and the upper limit will be £100,000.

2. The intermediate track will sit immediately above (a) the Online Solutions Court and (b) the residue of the fast track.

3. There will be a number of specified criteria for allocation to the track (see 3.2 above).

4. The Court will have the power to re-allocate to the track.

5. Clinical negligence claims above £25,000 will seldom be suitable for the intermediate track, unless both breach of duty and causation have been admitted at an early stage. The multi-track will be the normal track for clinical negligence claims above £25,000.

6. Band 1 will be for the least complex cases in the intermediate track. A simple claim over the fast track limit, where there is only one issue and the trial will take a day or less, would generally be suitable for that band: for example, many debt claims or quantum only personal injury claims would be suitable for Band 1. Band 4 will be for the most complex cases in the intermediate track: Examples may be disputes about family businesses or boundary disputes between neighbours, where the disputed land has no great value. Employers' liability disease claims where there are serious issues of fact/law and the trial is likely to last three days. Bands 2 and 3 will be the 'normal' bands for intermediate track cases, with the more straightforward cases going into Band 2 and the more complex cases going into Band 3.

7. Pre-action process. The pre-action protocols should be amended to require the parties to endeavour to agree pre-action: (a) the appropriate track for cases and (b) in respect of intermediate track cases, the appropriate band. Claimants should state their proposals in this regard in the letter of claim. Defendants should do the same in the letter of response.

8. Exempt personal injury litigation from the proposed disclosure rules in the intermediate track. Standard disclosure will be the normal order in personal injury cases.

9. How will the four-column grid be used in personal injury cases? Straightforward cases, where only one issue (such as quantum) is in dispute, will generally go into Band 1. Cases where both liability and quantum are in dispute will generally go into Band 2 or Band 3. Cases where there are serious issues on breach, causa-

tion and quantum (but which still fall within the intermediate track) will go into Band 4.

10. A Defendant's failure to beat claimant's Part 36 offer – if the defendant fails to beat an effective claimant offer under CPR Part 36, for the reasons set out in chapter 5 above and subject to the same caveats, it tentatively proposes that there should be a 30% or 40% uplift on costs rather than indemnity costs.

11. Part 8 proceedings will not initially be included. There should be FRC for (a) applications to approve settlements for children and protected parties and (b) costs only proceedings, in respect of intermediate track cases.

12. The reforms once implemented will be reviewed in four years time.

CHAPTER THREE
FURTHER FIXED COSTS IN EL, PL AND TRAVEL CLAIMS AND MITIGATING THE EFFECTS

The Jackson 2017 supplemental report sets out:-

"1.4 The proposed Online Solutions Court. Lord Justice Briggs has recommended the creation of an Online Solutions Court, which will deal with cases up to a value of £25,000. ***Personal injury, clinical negligence, possession, intellectual property and housing disrepair claims will be excluded from the Online Solutions Court****: see Briggs LJ's Final Report, paragraphs 6.95-6.102. It therefore follows that the Online Solutions Court will scoop up some of the current fast track cases and assign to them strictly limited recoverable costs. But a large rump of the fast track will remain in place under the rules proposed in this chapter".*

Extending fixed recoverable costs across the whole fast track

3.1 The time has come to finish the task. The time has surely come to complete the introduction of FRC across the fast track, not to keep kicking the issue into the long grass. ***There is now a general acceptance that FRC should be extended horizontally across the whole of the fast track****. The Bar Council, the Personal Injury Bar Association and many others accept that principle, although they add caveats and points on the details. The South East Circuit ("SEC") in their written submissions state:*

"The SEC can see that fixed costs on the fast-track (claims of up to £25,000) is probably appropriate and, perhaps, desirable. This is because fast-track claims:

a. Are inherently simpler, otherwise they would have been allocated to the multi-track.

b. Are subject to simpler procedural rules and thus involve less and more predictable work, making the idea of broad-brush fixed costs more just and legitimate amongst stake-holders.
c. Are at greater risk of disproportionate costs given the relatively low value of the claims.
d. Constitute the great majority of non-small claims work. According to Civil Justice Quarterly Statistics, 80% of non-small claims cases are allocated to the fast-track."

I agree with that view and recommend that all recoverable costs in the fast track should be fixed.

3.2 Fast track cases for which we do not yet have FRC. We do not yet have FRC for non- personal injury claims. Also, there are categories of personal injury claims for which FRC are not yet in place. In particular:

- ***Holiday sickness claims.*** *These are growing in frequency and are the subject of much discussion in the media. [**The Government has recently announced an intention to introduce FRC for holiday sickness claims. I support that proposal, but suggest that it should be implemented as part of a comprehensive FRC regime.**] Appendix 4 plots claimant costs against damages received in 79 such cases. On the basis of the evidence received during this review, I would suggest that the FRC for such claims (when pursued individually) [Multi-party actions in holiday sickness cases should proceed in the multi-track, as now] should be the same as for RTA personal injury cases.*
- *Employers' liability disease ("ELD"). In recent years, most ELD cases in the fast track have been claims for noise induced hearing loss ("NIHL").*
- *Other fast track personal injury claims which are excluded from the Protocols for Low Value RTA, ELA and PL Claims.*

3.3 NIHL. A working party set up by the Civil Justice Council ("CJC"), whose members include claimant and defendant representatives, has put forward proposals for FRC in respect of NIHL claims which remain in the fast track. This agreement was reached fol-

lowing a mediation. A summary of the NIHL mediated agreement is at Appendix 11. The agreement reached also includes a detailed bespoke procedure for NIHL claims, which is not appended but builds on principles of transparency and early information exchange between the parties. Its key recommendations include new forms of letter of claim and letter of response, with the letter of claim accompanied by an audiogram from an accredited audiologist as objective evidence of the claimant's level of hearing. Post-issue there should be specialist standard directions. Certain types of more complex claim have been excluded but the agreement is believed to cover the vast majority of fast track NIHL claims. The final report is with the CJC for approval and I anticipate that this will soon be published by the CJC.

3.4 Lack of data for non-personal injury cases. Despite the best efforts of the assessors and myself, very little data are available in respect of the costs of non-personal injury fast track cases, apart from non-personal injury RTA claims. By definition, such cases fall outside the costs management regime. So there are no court approved budgets for us to look at. The Bar Council's online survey only included two non-personal injury fast track cases. The Housing Law Practitioners Association ("HLPA") has supplied details of 83 fast track disrepair cases, which the FTWG and I have examined with care. These data give an impression of recoverable costs in recent cases where courts have applied the new proportionality rule. But they do not provide evidence relating to agreed costs at settlement on a sufficient volume of claims to allow any degree of statistical confidence about the average amounts recovered on such cases.

3.5 Does that mean we can never fix costs for non-personal injury fast track cases? No. We should put forward what seem to be reasonable figures for each category of case, having regard to:
(i) the proportionality factors set out in CPR rule 44.3(5);
(ii) such data as are available;
(iii) the experience of the assessors;
(iv) the costs of conducting personal injury cases of comparable complexity.

3.6 London weighting. The current FRC rules in the fast track provide for a 12.5% uplift on fixed costs payable to a party who lives in the London area and instructs a legal representative who practises in the London area: see CPR rule 45.29C(2), rule 45.29F(5) and to the extended FRC regime proposed in this chapter.

3.7 Contractual entitlement to costs. Some contracts contain express provisions governing costs in the event of litigation. Examples of such contracts may be mortgages, guarantees or leases. Often, particularly in the case of mortgages, the Court will not be asked to make any costs order at all as the mortgagee will recover its costs from the proceeds of sale of the property. The CPR expressly provide that a mortgagee is not obliged to apply for a costs order: see CPR rule 44.5 and Practice Direction 44, paragraph 7.1. Such costs can also be recovered by a pleaded claim for a contractual indemnity. Even where the Court is asked to make a costs order under the discretionary power in section 51 of the Senior Courts Act 1981, the effect of CPR rule 44.5 is that in contractual costs cases the Court will make an indemnity costs order, unless the contract expressly provides otherwise. This reflects the substantive law position, as indicated by Gomba Holdings (UK) Ltd v Minories Finance Ltd [1993] Ch 171, Church Commissioners v Ibrahim [1997] EGLR 13 and Chaplair Holdings (UK) Ltd v Kumari [2015] EWCA Civ 798, that the contractual entitlement is free from the restraints imposed by procedural rules on recovery of costs and will be free from the FRC regimes suggested in this report. The court will enforce the contractual right, subject to its equitable power to disallow unreasonable expenses. There is nothing in the rule making powers in respect of the CPR which enable the rules to exclude or override a contractual entitlement. Primary legislation would be required to alter that position. Although there has been some discussion of this issue at the seminars, the question whether the present position is satisfactory does not fall within my terms of reference. Wider policy issues are in play, such as what would be the effect on overall mortgage interest rates, if mortgagees could not provide for the contractual recovery of litigation costs. In this report, therefore, I do not address the question of contractual entitlement to costs.

3.8 Such cases remain in the fast track. The fact that one party has a contractual entitlement to costs does not prevent a case proceeding in the fast track. The case will be subject to the case management rules of CPR Part 28. If the party with a contractual entitlement to costs succeeds, then the costs position will be as set out in the preceding paragraph.

4 Noise induced hearing loss

4.1 The mediated agreement. As can be seen from appendix 11, the claimant and defendant representatives on the CJC working group have agreed a prescriptive process for dealing with NIHL claims and an accompanying grid of FRC. In my view, the agreement reached is a reasonable one and I endorse it.

4.2 Costs grid for NIHL claims. The agreed costs grid for NIHL claims, which I endorse, is as follows:

Proposed matrix of FRC for NIHL claims (applies to both claimant and defendant recoverable costs)

Stage:	***NIHL claims with value less than £25,000***
Pre-issue	*£4,000 + £500 per extra defendant (reduced by £1,000 if there is an early admission of liability or by £500 if settled before proceedings drafted)*
Post-issue, pre-allocation	*£5,650 + £830 uplift per extra defendant*
Post-allocation, pre-listing	*£7,306 + £1,161 uplift per extra defendant*
Post-listing, pre- trial	*£9,187 + £1,537 uplift per extra defendant*
Trial advocacy fee	*Not agreed*

In addition to the above, a fee of £1,280 is recoverable for restoring a company to the register.

4.3 Counsel's fees and trial advocacy fees. The CJC working group did not reach full agreement on these matters. I have considered the relevant material and the rival submissions made within the working group. I recommend that counsel's fees and trial advocacy fees in NIHL cases should be the same as those which I propose for 'Band 4' cases in the next section of this chapter. Almost all NIHL claims are low value. So, as set out below, the trial advocacy fee will generally be £1,380.

5 The remainder of the fast track

5.1 Proposed matrix of FRC and paradigm cases. Drawing on the work of the FTWG, I propose that all fast track cases be placed into four bands of complexity, Band 1 being the least complex and Band 4 being the most complex. The following are paradigm cases for each band:

Band 1: RTA non-personal injury claims (popularly known as 'bent metal' claims). Band 2: RTA personal injury claims.
Band 3: ELA and PL accident claims.
Band 4: ELD claims (non-NIHL) and the most complex fast track claims.

5.2 A fuller list of cases suitable for each band. I propose the following:

Band 1: RTA non-personal injury, defended debt cases.
Band 2: RTA personal injury (within Protocol), holiday sickness claims.
Band 3: RTA personal injury (outside Protocol), ELA, PL, tracked possession claims, housing disrepair, other money claims.
Band 4: ELD claims (other than NIHL), any particularly complex tracked possession claims or housing disrepair claims, property disputes, professional negligence claims and other claims at the top end of the fast track.

5.3 At the allocation stage, the court must have discretion to move individual claims between those bands having regard to the nature of the individual case. Judges should exercise this discretion sparingly and bearing in mind the proportionality factors set out in CPR rule 44.3(5). Any case of particular complexity does not belong in the fast track at all.

5.4 Recoverable costs. I propose that the recoverable costs for each band be as follows: Table 5.2

Matrix of FRC for fast track claims (applies to both claimant and defendant recoverable costs)

	Complexity Band			
Stage:	*1*	*2*	*3*	*4*
Pre-issue £1,001-£5,000		*£104 + 20% of damages*	*£988 + 17.5% of damages*	
Pre-issue £5,001-£10,000		*£1,144 + 15% of damages over £5,000*	*£1,929 + 12.5% of damages over £5,000*	*£2,250 + 15% of damages + £440 per extra defendant*
Pre-issue £10,001-£25,000	*£500*	*£2,007 + 10% of damages over £10,000*	*£2,600 + 10% of damages over £10,000*	
Post-issue, pre- allocation	*£1,850*	*£1,206 + 20% of damages*	*£2,735 + 20% of damages*	*£2,575 + 40% of damages + £660 per extra defendant*
Post-allocation, pre-listing	*£2,200*	*£1,955 + 20% of damages*	*£3,484 + 25% of damages*	*£5,525 + 40% of damages + £660 per extra defendant*
Post-listing, pre- trial	*£3,250*	*£2,761 + 20% of damages*	*£4,451 + 30% of damages*	*£6,800 + 40% of damages + £660 per extra defendant*
Trial advocacy fee [11]	*a. £500 b. £710 c. £1,070 d. £1,705*	*a. £500 b. £710 c. £1,070 d. £1,705*	*a. £500 b. £710 c. £1,070 d. £1,705*	*a. £1,380 b. £1,380 c. £1,800 d. £2,500*

[11] a. claim value up to £3,000; b. claim value £3,001 to £10,000; c. claim value £10,001 to £15,000; d. claim value £15,001 to £25,000.

The figures in all boxes are cumulative, except for the trial advocacy fees shown in the bottom line. The word "damages" is used as shorthand for debt, liquidated sum or other monetary relief. There is obviously some difficulty in applying the above table to claims for, or including, non-monetary relief. The court must, I am afraid assign a value to such relief. I propose that a claim for a declaration or injunction should be treated as the equivalent of a claim for £10,000, with the court having power to vary that figure upwards or downwards. [For example, in a housing disrepair claim where the defendant is ordered to carry out repairs with a value of £20,000, the injunction requiring such works should be treated as if it were an award of £20,000.]

If the claimant succeeds, the specified percentage applies to the relief recovered. If the defendant succeeds, the specified percentage applies to the claim defeated, as valued in the particulars of claim.

5.5 How are the figures in the table derived? The figures in ***Band 1*** *are based on an analysis of data from Taylor Rose TTKW13 in which fast track RTA claims, with zero general damages but positive special damages between £10,000 and £25,000 in value, were summarised by the chronological stage of litigation at settlement. The mean amounts of recovered base costs were estimated, and adjusted to take account of efficiency savings from fixed costs. These adjustments were necessary to make the figures comparable with the other fast track fixed cost bands.*

5.6 The figures in ***Bands 2 and 3*** *are the existing figures for fast track pre-trial fixed costs in personal injury cases with an uplift of 4% to take account of inflation from July 2013 (when those figures were set) to July 2016. I appreciate that a few of those figures have an earlier origin than 2013, but a policy decision was taken in July*

2013 to re-adopt those earlier figures. The figure of 4% is derived from the Services Producer Price Index.

5.7 The figures in ***Band 4*** *are based on an analysis of Taylor Rose TTKW data, recording the claimants' costs agreed in a large volume of fast track ELD claims. The figures have been adjusted to take account of efficiency savings from fixed costs. These cases are of comparable complexity to the heaviest non-personal injury claims in the fast track.*

At the allocation stage, the court must have discretion to move individual claims between those bands having regard to the nature of the individual case. Judges should exercise this discretion sparingly and bearing in mind the proportionality factors set out in CPR rule 44.3(5).

5.13 Interim applications and preliminary issues. The costs of any applications properly made (e.g. because the other party is in default) should be recovered separately. There are fixed costs for such applications under CPR rule 45.29H. I propose that in NIHL and Band 4 cases, the provision in CPR rule 45.29H(1) "one half of the applicable Type A and Type B costs" should be amended to "two thirds of the applicable Type A and Type B costs". The fixed recoverable fee for an interim injunction application should be £750.

5.18 Housing claims. The principal categories of housing claims are:

1. *Defending claims for possession, including mortgage repossession.*
2. *Claims for unlawful eviction.*
3. *Homelessness applications, including County Court appeals.*
4. ***Claims for breach of repairing obligations.***
5. *Judicial review in respect of housing law issues.*

The HLPA say that they are particularly concerned about housing disrepair claims because these seldom qualify for legal aid. I understand from one of my assessors, who has experience of managing disrepair cases in the fast track, that the FRC regime proposed above would be satisfactory for most disrepair claims. ***Most such claims***

would fit into either Band 3 or Band 4. *Nevertheless, in certain of the cases cited by the HLPA, the recovered costs are higher than the proposed FRC (even allowing for the fact that the HLPA figures include VAT and disbursements). Possibly these are cases which ought not to have been in the fast track at all or possibly they are exceptional cases where the escape clause might be invoked (as to which see below). It is difficult to say without having the details of individual cases.*

5.21 Fast track procedure. The standard directions in Practice Direction 28 may require modification in Band 4 and NIHL cases. For example, in NIHL cases the mediated agreement envisages a set of directions capable of covering the use of experts in different disciplines to deal separately with issues of liability and quantum: those directions would typically allow for questions to be put to the claimant's quantum expert and for the joint instruction of a liability expert. Band 4 cases may require different modifications, but always within the context of the case remaining in the fast track. This is something that the Rule Committee will need to consider in due course.

5.22 Assessment of costs. In most cases, the assessment of recoverable costs should be a straightforward exercise, not requiring judicial input. ***In so far as there is any dispute, the court will assess costs. If the case goes to trial, the judge will summarily assess costs at the end of the hearing. In cases which do not go to trial, there should be a shortened form of detailed assessment, of the kind described in the last sentence of Practice Direction 47, paragraph 5.7, with a provisional assessment fee cap of – say – £500.***

Key Points:-

1. Fixed costs in the fast track will extend to non personal injury work such as housing disrepair and all personal injury work as well as NIHL and holiday/travel claims.

2. There is a table of fixed costs (as above) for NIHL cases.

3. At the allocation stage, the court must have discretion to move individual claims between those bands having regard to the nature of the individual case. Judges should exercise this discretion sparingly and bearing in mind the proportionality factors set out in CPR rule 44.3(5).

4. Costs of interim applications will remain fixed as per CPR 45.29H. In NIHL and Band 4 cases, the provision in CPR rule 45.29H(1) "one half of the applicable Type A and Type B costs" should be amended to "two thirds of the applicable Type A and Type B costs".

5. Housing disrepair claims would fall into band 3 or 4.

6. Who will decide on the bands and when? The pre-action protocols should be amended to require the parties to endeavour to agree pre-action: (a) the appropriate track for cases and (b) in respect of fast track cases, the appropriate band. Claimants should state their proposals in this regard in the letter of claim. Defendants should do the same in the letter of response. If the case reaches allocation stage, the district judge or master should allocate in the usual way and (for fast track cases) specify the band if that is in dispute. Either party could challenge that decision by an application on paper under CPR rule 3.3(5)–(6). It is proposed that the unsuccessful party on such an application should incur a costs liability of £150. If the case settles before issue or before allocation, then the band allocation decision should fall to the judge assessing costs if there is disagreement between the parties.

7. Provisional assessment will apply to all such cases.

The Jackson report makes some interesting observations from the discussions with PI Lawyers on the subject:-

18.5 The APIL conference provided an opportunity for me to talk informally to many highly experienced personal injury and clinical negligence lawyers. This informal feedback revealed:

(i) The proposed intermediate track will catch very few cases if it is limited to cases where each party only has one oral expert. Furthermore, 'one oral expert cases' will not need three days. It would be more realistic to limit the intermediate track to cases where there are not more than two oral experts on each side and the trial will take not more than three days.
(ii) Multiple defendant cases would be unsuitable for the intermediate track, unless liability is admitted and the only issue is quantum.
(iii) Quite a few solicitors would be content to have FRC in personal injury cases (but not clinical negligence cases) where the claim is up to £75,000 or £100,000, provided that (a) there is a streamlined procedure and (b) the figures are right.
(iv) An FRC regime should be designed to reward defendants who admit liability early.
(v) If an FRC regime is introduced, lawyers are likely to innovate and find ways of working within it.
(vi) It is not right to say that all RTA cases or all 'bent metal' cases are simple. In cases where there is a claim for vehicle damage, there is almost always a personal injury claim as well.
(vii) In any FRC regime there must be clarity about escape provisions.
(viii) Several APIL members are involved in developing a special process for clinical negligence claims up to £25,000. They believe that if a prescriptive procedure for such cases is developed collaboratively with the DoH, then it could be combined with an FRC regime for cases up to £25,000.
(ix) In Scotland, there is now an "All-Scotland Sheriff Personal Injury Court" with streamlined procedures. This has a lower threshold of £1,000/£5,000. Personal injury cases cannot start in the Court of Session (the Scottish equivalent of the High Court) unless they have a value above £100,000, albeit they follow the same procedures. Gordon Dalyell (Vice-President of APIL) says that the regime of the Sheriff Personal Injury Court generally works well,

although there have been some issues relating to administrative resources.

CHAPTER FOUR CHANGES TO COSTS BUDGETING AND THE EFFECTS ON COSTS BUDGETING

The New Form Bill of Costs Keynote Address to the Law Society's Civil Litigation Conference 21 April 2016 LJ Jackson said:- https://www.judiciary.gov.uk/wp-content/uploads/2016/04/speech-lj-jackson-bill-of-costs.pdf

> *2.1 The problem. The current form bill of costs has a long and distinguished pedigree. It is based upon the style of a Victorian account book. Despite those historic virtues, the format is neither helpful nor appropriate in the twenty first century.* ***The current form of bill makes it relatively easy for a receiving party to disguise or even hide what has gone on. What is required is a bill which (a) gives relevant information to the court and to the paying party and (b) is transparent. PR*** *chapter 53 highlighted these issues and invited consultees to give their views.*
>
> *2.2 Views during the Costs Review consultation. Most of those consulted endorsed the criticisms set out above. The current bill of costs is cumbersome, time consuming and expensive to produce. It is opaque, giving no clear information to the reader as to why costs were incurred or even the underlying work done. The information about time spent on documents is particularly difficult to decode.* ***The current form of bill is an anachronism that makes no use of time-recording software.***
>
> *THE CURRENT PROPOSALS*
>
> *3.1 Hutton Committee proposals. After the publication of the FR, the development of a new bill of costs passed to an ad-hoc working party set up under the auspices of Jeremy Morgan QC, one of my assessors during the Costs Review, to take the project forward. Alexander*

Hutton QC took over responsibilities as chair on Jeremy Morgan's retirement and the working party is now commonly known as "The Hutton Committee".

3.2 The Hutton Committee, after a considerable amount of effort and hard graft, have produced a new format bill of costs which is built on three integrated pieces of work.

3.3 The J-Codes. First, they have created J-Codes – a standardised way of capturing time-recorded information adapted from the UTBMS which is used for eBilling in the United States and US law firms operating in the United Kingdom. The J-Codes work by identifying the Precedent H phase in which work is undertaken (e.g. Pre-Action), what task is being worked on (e.g. Investigation of the facts or law) and the type of activity being undertaken (e.g. Planning, researching or drafting). The J-Codes were endorsed by the Master of the Rolls, Senior Costs Judge Peter Hurst and myself on 30th July 2014. They have now been ratified by the body with oversight of the UTBMS, the LEDES Oversight Committee.

3.4 The electronic spreadsheet. Secondly, there is a multi-purpose electronic Excel spreadsheet. ***This allows for a firm's time-recording data to be fed into it automatically and to create a bill of costs from it. It is possible to sort the data in a number of ways (by phase, by date or by the type of work being done). From this base you can generate a bill showing the full amount of the actual costs, which the client must pay. You can also generate a bill showing the costs recoverable from the other side. This requires adjustments, to strip out items payable by the client but not permissible as recoverable costs. The electronic spreadsheet can produce a bill for either detailed or summary assessment.***

3.5 The finished bill. Thirdly, there is the finished version of the bill - this condenses all the information contained in the spreadsheet into a clear and legible format. It makes it possible for the judge or the paying party to examine the bill in varying levels of

generality and with ease of comparison with the costs budget. Although the full bill will be in electronic form only (as it will have too many columns to print in A4) and designed primarily for use on screen, a shortened printed version can easily be made from it. Both will need to be served. A finished version of the print bill, including example data, is available as Precedent AA, attached to PD 51L (White Book pages 1627-1645) and available on the Ministry of Justice website.

3.6 Consultation and criticism. The Hutton Committee conducted a consultation on their proposals and received a number of critical responses. Four key strands of criticism have emerged from them, namely:
a) The proposed bill is too expensive to implement;
b) The proposed bill is too complex to work with;
c) The proposed bill is too time-consuming to transfer work done before J-codesinto the new format; and
d) The proposed bill is too prescriptive in using J-Codes.

3.7 Decision of the CPRC. The CPRC established a voluntary pilot for the proposed new bill of costs, commencing in October 2015. Practice Direction 51L sets out the rules governing the voluntary pilot. The original plan was that the voluntary pilot would end this month and that a mandatory pilot would start. However, at their December 2015 meeting, the CPRC decided to extend the lifespan of the voluntary pilot until December 2016. It was agreed that the proposals warranted "careful further consideration" and "that it was too soon for any decision to be taken."

3.8 Where next for the new bill? The CPRC were right to be cautious. This is an important reform, affecting the professions and the judiciary as a whole, which we need to get right. However, there is now a state of deadlock. We need practical proposals to break the deadlock and advance the discussion.

3.9 To that end, I put forward this paper as one such proposal. In Section 4, I will examine the criticisms made of the current proposals and whether they have any merit or not. Then, in Section 5, I will suggest what can be done to address those criticisms which have any force behind them as well as a number of other matters which could be implemented.

3.10 Interface with the Briggs reforms. More and more work is now being done electronically. The Briggs Review is carefully examining the structure of the civil courts and the scope for electronic working. That review is likely to lead to major reform. The traditional bill of costs, based on the style of a Victorian account book, is already inappropriate for the digital age. It can only become more so as the IT revolution finally reaches the civil courts.

5. THE WAY FORWARD

5.1 A modest proposal. There is a practical solution to the present quandary. I suggest that the way forward is to revise the current proposals, preserving the work of the Hutton Committee while allowing for greater flexibility in the new bill.

5.2 The Hutton Committee's proposed version of the bill should be adopted as the new bill format, albeit with the references to the J-Codes removed. The CPR should allow practitioners to prepare that bill in any manner of their choosing; whether with the assistance of J-Codes, automatically generated by an Excel spreadsheet or by hand.

5.3 A digital copy of the bill should be served on the court and the paying party along with an electronic spreadsheet, which clearly and accurately details the work done in the course of litigation, following the Precedent H stages. This should be in the same format of phase/task/activity and adopt the Precedent H guidance for what work falls in a given phase. Time entries can either be generated automatically by time- recording software or inputted manually by those who prefer to record their work done on paper. For those using J-Codes, the Hutton Committee spreadsheet provides an excellent tool for preparing the bill.

5.4 Court IT. It is important that any new IT for the civil courts should have the capacity to receive electronically both costs budgets and bills of costs in the new form. I would respectfully urge those designing new hardware and software for the civil courts to take this into account.

5.5 The above proposal has three key elements to commend it.

(i) First, we have a new format bill which meets the three criteria set out at paragraph 2.3 above and the Recommendations in the FR. The new format bill integrates with costs budgeting and Precedent H. It can be generated automatically by time- recording software. It provides a framework for software providers to create tools for the professions.
(ii) Secondly, it makes good use of the excellent work of the Hutton Committee. Indeed, it would not be possible without it. While revising the proposals will mean that the current version of the spreadsheet and the J-Codes are not an essential part of the scheme, their value will be preserved for those who adopt J-Codes. As suggested above at paragraph 4.16, the professions should give serious consideration to them.
(iii) Thirdly, it sidesteps much of the criticism which gave rise to the present delays. The print version of the bill and the accompanying spreadsheet are not radical innovations. Nor do they involve significant cost. They require only a basic level of computer literacy and an understanding of how to present information clearly.

5.6 Retrospective application? One of the more serious criticisms is the argument that retrospective application of the new format bill and of J-Codes would increase the cost of bill preparation dramatically.

5.7 The proposal above diminishes the seriousness of this criticism. There is, however, a complete solution to the problem. The CPRC should choose a future date for the implementation of the new bill. ***Work done before this date may be recorded in the old system and with the old format bill. Work done after this date should be done in the new format bill. There will be no retrospective imposition***

and no need to go through historic information, trying to apply the phase/task/activity format retrospectively. *May I suggest that the new form bill of costs should be mandatory for all work done on or after 1st October 2017? The voluntary pilot under PD 51L could be extended until that date.*

5.8 Fixed costs for bill preparation In addition, I invite consideration of a proposal to cap or fix the recoverable costs of preparing the bill. The receiving party should only expect to recover up to a certain amount for the preparation of the bill – possibly expressed as a % figure of the total value of the assessed bill.

5.9 Does any of this matter if we have fixed costs for the multi-track? ***The only way to control costs effectively is to do so in advance, i.e. before the money is spent. That means either fixed costs or costs management.*** *There is room for debate as to where the boundary between those two regimes should lie. It is a mistake to think that the recent proposals for fixed costs makes the new format bill an irrelevance. This is for three reasons:*

(i) *If there is a fixed costs regime (of the kind I have previously suggested) for the multi-track, it will only go up to a certain level and it will only apply to assessment on the standard basis. There will still be many bills of costs requiring detailed assessment.*
(ii) *In view of the vociferous opposition to fixed costs, it is uncertain when and up to what level fixed costs will be introduced.*
(iii) ***Even in cases subject to fixed costs, contemporaneous electronic time-recording under phase, task and activity (such as with J-Codes) would provide invaluable internal management data to enable firms (a) to maximise their profits and (b) to run those cases as efficiently as possible. This will be particularly important if the new regime prescribes fixed costs for each phase, as previously recommended.***

5.10 Conclusion. If this proposal finds favour with the CPRC – and with the professions more generally – then I suggest that the best way forward is to take three steps:

(i) First, create a version of the print bill and spreadsheet which removes references to the J-Codes. The bulk of work has already been done by the Hutton Committee and it does not require major surgery.
(ii) Secondly, set a date for when the CPRC will decide whether to implement the new bill of costs (subject to appropriate modifications). Invite interested parties to send in representations on the new bill to a CPRC sub-committee, which can report back at that meeting.
(iii) Extend the voluntary pilot under PD 51L until such time as the new form bill of costs becomes mandatory.

5.11 Preliminary draft of the new bill. A possible preliminary draft of the new bill is attached to this paper for consideration.

5.12 Regardless of whether this particular proposal is accepted or not, one thing does need to be kept in mind: the status quo is of no benefit to anyone. Investment decisions on time-recording software are being deferred. The work of the Hutton Committee has been left to lie fallow. Most egregiously, we still have a bill of costs that was identified as being seriously deficient many years ago.

5.13 This is not intended as a criticism of the CPRC's decision last December. The consultation responses rightly gave them pause for thought. However, the obstacles are not insurmountable. The Hutton Committee has designed a new bill that is fit for purpose. With the appropriate rule changes and practical steps in the implementation process, the concerns can be addressed.

Key Points:-

1. The new system will allow data to be pulled from the firm's case management system to create the bill.

2. The system is due to be implemented in April 2018.

3. For those who have already invested in software, it is possible to make these systems J- Code compatible with a relatively small amount of changes and costs.

4. The Hutton Committee's proposed version of the bill should be adopted as the new bill format, albeit with the references to the J-Codes removed. The CPR should allow practitioners to prepare that bill in any manner of their choosing; whether with the assistance of J-Codes, automatically generated by an Excel spreadsheet or by hand.

5. A digital copy of the bill should be served on the court and the paying party along with an electronic spreadsheet, which clearly and accurately details the work done in the course of litigation, following the Precedent H stages. This should be in the same format of phase/task/activity and adopt the Precedent H guidance for what work falls in a given phase. Time entries can either be generated automatically by time-recording software or inputted manually by those who prefer to record their work done on paper. For those using J-Codes, the Hutton Committee spreadsheet provides an excellent tool for preparing the bill.

6. The drafting of bills in the new format will not be retrospective for work done under the old system.

7. Costs incurred after 6th April 2018 will have to be shown in the new format for virtually all multi-track bills and practitioners need to understand what is required. For each item in the new bill a phase code, task code, activity/expense code must be assigned. There are 14 phases, 41 tasks, 10 activities and 13 expenses codes to choose from.

CHAPTER FIVE
CHANGES TO THE SMALL CLAIMS TRACK IN PI CLAIMS FOR EL/ PL AND TRAVEL CLAIMS

PI Lawyers have known for some time now that there are likely going to be increases to the small claims track in 2018/2019.

The Jackson report on the issue sets out:-

> *3.10 Whiplash reforms. On 23rd February 2017, the Government published part one of its responses to the consultation, "Reforming the soft tissue injury ('whiplash') claims process", which closed on 6th January 2017.15 This included a number of reforms, including the introduction of a tariff of fixed compensation for pain, suffering and loss of amenity for injuries with a duration of less than two years.* ***Further reforms include a ban on settlement of claims without medical evidence, increasing the small claims limit for RTA related personal injury claims to £5,000, and increasing the small claims limit for all other types of personal injury claims to £2,000.*** *The current limit for these types of claim is £1,000. The aim of these reforms is to disincentivise minor, exaggerated and fraudulent road traffic accident related soft-tissue claims, leading to projected overall savings to insurers of £1bn. The Government included clauses on these reforms in the Prison and Court Reform Bill, before the June General Election necessitated the dissolution of Parliament. In the Queen's Speech on 21st June, the new Government stated its intention to proceed with whiplash reform by a new Civil Liability Bill.*

Changes to Holiday Claims in 2018

An MOJ paper on holiday sickness claims dated October 2017 at: https://www.gov.uk/government/uploads/system/uploads/attachment_data/file/652419/gastric-illness-call-for-evidence.pdf sets out:-

> *"These are personal injury (PI) public liability (PL) claims, generally for food poisoning/gastric illness, which defendants say are often brought two or more years after the holiday in question (the limitation period is three years). They appear to be generally for relatively low damages individually (appearing to range upwards from around £800 per person, but can be combined for families or groups). There is a concern that the claim is easy to make with very little or no evidence, and this can create cost for the travel industry in defending the claim, even if they believe there is no merit in it. A particular concern is that the claimant's legal costs of dealing with these claims (paid by a losing defendant) are not fixed, as they have been since 2013 for other similar claims. This is because the breach of duty occurs outside England and Wales.*
>
> ***8. The Regulations ascribe liability to the tour operator for what occurred abroad. However, as the tour operator is based in England and Wales, it does not seem right that – albeit that the incident itself occurred abroad – that these claims should not be subject to the same fixed costs which would apply to an identical claim arising in England and Wales, not least because any extra work, when compared with a similar PI claim arising from an accident or alleged breach of duty occurring in England and Wales, would only fall to defendants who may need to liaise with, or take instructions from, the overseas provider (resort or hotel).***
>
> *9. Moreover, FRC provide certainty in the amount of costs that a losing party would have to pay and would reduce the financial burden of defending such claims, which is ultimately passed on to the consumer.*

10. Extending FRC would be effected by amending the Pre-Action Protocol for 'fast-track' (that is, under £25k damages) Employers' Liability and PL claims (the EL/PL PAP). Although the current concern is around GI claims – and irrespective of the reported disproportionate increase in the volume of GI claims - there would appear to be no justification for not extending FRC to cover all fast track PI PL package holiday claims. In particular, there is a real risk that taking action on GI claims alone could simply result in an unfounded increase in other types of holiday claims.

11. We are therefore proposing to extend the current FRC that apply to PL claims in England and Wales to those arising abroad under the Regulations. Following the Call for Evidence we would hope to be able to finalise any revisions to the EL/PL PAP quickly so that any changes can apply to all new claims from April 2018.

12. This approach is in line with wider Government policy which is to extend FRC where possible in civil litigation. Most, but not all, low value PI claims are now covered by FRC, and other initiatives are in train.

13. Most recently, on 31 July, Lord Justice Jackson published his report on extending FRC much more widely5. He recommended6 that FRC should be extended to cover holiday sickness claims. However, he recommended that the FRC should be at RTA rather than PL rates. That is something that we will consider in any consultation on his wider recommendations, but at this stage we are proposing to fix them at PL rates, as they would be if the incident occurred in England and Wales.

(iii) amendments to Pre-Action Protocol for Low Value Personal Injury (Employers' Liability and Public Liability) Claims (EL/PL PAP)

14. The main proposal is to amend the EL/PL PAP to ensure that it - and so, in turn, the FRC provisions in Part 45 of the Civil Procedure Rules (CPR) - would apply to PI claims where the Regulations are engaged. An amendment to Part 45 would also be required to give effect to this. In addition, some further amendments would be required to reflect what is understood to be current industry practice when dealing with such claims at the pre-action stage. We consider that amendment to the following provisions, which would only apply to PI claims where the Regulations are engaged, would be required.

Key Points:-

1. The small claims track for RTA claims will increase to £5,000.

2. The small claims track for EL/PL claims will increase to £2,000.

3. The implementation date is yet to be determined but is likely to be April or October 2019 for RTA, EL and PL claims.

4. Extending FRC would be effected by amending the Pre-Action Protocol for 'fast-track' (that is, under £25k damages) Employers' Liability and PL claims (the EL/PL PAP), for all package travel cases.

CHAPTER SIX
TARIFFS IN RTA CLAIMS AND RUNNING CLAIMS UNDER THE NEW SYSTEM

Perhaps one the biggest casualties of the PI reforms will be RTA claims. It is proposed from 2019 the following table of costs will apply to RTA claims, as set out in the MOJ consultation paper at https://www.-gov.uk/government/uploads/system/uploads/attachment_data/file/593431/part-1-response-to-reforming-soft-tissue-injury-claims.pdf:-

Injury Duration	2015 average payment for PSLA – uplifted to take account of JCG uplift (industry data)	Judicial College Guideline (JCG) amounts (13th edition) Published September 2015	New tariff amounts
0–3 months	£1,750	A few hundred pounds to £2,050	£225
4–6 months	£2,150	£2,050 to £3,630	£450
7–9 months	£2,600	£2,050 to £3,630	£765
10–12 months	£3,100	£2,050 to £3,630	£1,190
13–15 months	£3,500	£3,630 to £6,600	£1,820
16–18 months	£3,950	£3,630 to £6,600	£2,660
19–24 months	£4,500	£3,630 to £6,600	£3,725

Key Points from the Consultation Paper:-

1. A tariff of fixed compensation for PSLA for whiplash claims with a duration of 0-24 months;

2. An ability for the judiciary to decrease the tariff in the event of contributory negligence or to increase the tariff by up to 20% in exceptional circumstances;

3. A ban on offering and requesting pre-med offers;

4. The tariff will cover both whiplash claims and minor psychological claims, rather than having separate amounts as consulted on. The report said:- "*The government accepts that the definition should not cover more serious psychological illnesses, for example, depression and post-traumatic stress disorder, which are diagnosable using international standards. The government therefore proposes to limit the scope of this measure to minor psychological injuries, such as 'travel anxiety' and 'shock'.*"

   "The government is of the view that low-value personal injury claims are not so complex as to routinely require a lawyer. Raising the small claims limit to cover PSLA claims of up to £5,000 will not preclude claimants from engaging legal representation, but would mean that they would in future be responsible for paying for their own legal costs if they so choose."

5. It would seem unlikely that post reforms, RTA will be a market that most Solicitors will not be able to operate in, unless they undertake volume claims. The DBA Regulations 2013 prevent taking more than 25% of damages in personal injury claims, so this may need to change.

DBA 2013 Regulations

The 2013 Regulations set out:-

2013 No. 000 - LEGAL SERVICES, ENGLAND AND WALES
The Damages-Based Agreements Regulations 2013
Made
***

Coming into force
1st April 2013

The Lord Chancellor in exercise of the powers conferred by sections 58AA(4) and (5) and 120(3) of the Courts and Legal Services Act 1990(1), having consulted in accordance with section 58AA(6) of that Act, makes the following Regulations, a draft of which has been laid before and approved by resolution of each House of Parliament in accordance with section 120(4)(2) of that Act.

Citation, commencement, interpretation and application
1.—(1) These Regulations may be cited as the Damages-Based Agreements Regulations 2013 and come into force on 1st April 2013.

(2) In these Regulations—
"the Act" means the Courts and Legal Services Act 1990;
"claim for personal injuries" has the same meaning as in Rule 2.3 of the Civil Procedure Rules 1998(3);
- *"client" means the person who has instructed the representative to provide advocacy services, litigation services (within section 119 of the Act) or claims management services (within the meaning of section 4(2)(b) of the Compensation Act 2006(4)) and is liable to make a payment for those services;*
- *"costs" means the total of the representative's time reasonably spent, in respect of the claim or proceedings, multiplied by the reasonable hourly rate of remuneration of the representative;*
- *"employment matter" means a matter that is, or could become, the subject of proceedings before an employment tribunal;*
- *"expenses" means disbursements incurred by the representative, including the expense of obtaining an expert's report and, in an employment matter only, counsel's fees;*
- *"payment" means that part of the sum recovered in respect of the claim or damages awarded that the client agrees to pay the representative, and excludes expenses but includes, in respect of any claim or proceedings to which these regulations apply other than an employment matter, any disbursements incurred by the representative in respect of counsel's fees;*

- *"representative" means the person providing the advocacy services, litigation services or claims management services to which the damages-based agreement relates.*

(3) Subject to paragraphs (4), (5) and (6), these Regulations shall apply to all damages-based agreements entered into on or after the date on which these Regulations come into force.

(4) Subject to paragraph (6), these Regulations shall not apply to any damages-based agreement to which section 57 of the Solicitors Act 1974(5) (non-contentious business agreements between solicitor and client) applies.

(5) In these Regulations—
(a) regulation 4 does not apply; and
(b) regulations 5, 6, 7 and 8 only apply,
to any damages-based agreement in respect of an employment matter.

(6) Where these Regulations relate to an employment matter, they apply to all damages-based agreements signed on or after the date on which these Regulations come into force.

Revocation of 2010 Regulations and transitional provision
2.—(1) Subject to paragraph (2), the Damages-Based Agreements Regulations 2010(6) ("the 2010 Regulations") are revoked.

(2) The 2010 Regulations shall continue to have effect in respect of any damages-based agreement to which those Regulations applied and which was signed before the date on which these Regulations come into force.

Requirements of an agreement in respect of all damages-based agreements
3. The requirements prescribed for the purposes of section 58AA(4)(c) of the Act are that the terms and conditions of a damages-based agreement must specify—

(a) the claim or proceedings or parts of them to which the agreement relates;
(b) the circumstances in which the representative's payment, expenses and costs, or part of them, are payable; and
(c) the reason for setting the amount of the payment at the level agreed, which, in an employment matter, shall include having regard to, where appropriate, whether the claim or proceedings is one of several similar claims or proceedings.

Payment in respect of claims or proceedings other than an employment matter
4.—(1) In respect of any claim or proceedings, other than an employment matter, to which these Regulations apply, a damages-based agreement must not require an amount to be paid by the client other than—
(a) the payment, net of—
(I) any costs (including fixed costs under Part 45 of the Civil Procedure Rules 1998); and
(ii) where relevant, any sum in respect of disbursements incurred by the representative in respect of counsel's fees,
that have been paid or are payable by another party to the proceedings by agreement or order; and
(b) any expenses incurred by the representative, net of any amount which has been paid or is payable by another party to the proceedings by agreement or order.

(2) In a claim for personal injuries—
(a) the only sums recovered by the client from which the payment shall be met are—
(I) general damages for pain, suffering and loss of amenity; and
(ii) damages for pecuniary loss other than future pecuniary loss,
net of any sums recoverable by the Compensation Recovery Unit of the Department for Work and Pensions; and
(b) subject to paragraph (4), a damages-based agreement must not provide for a payment above an amount which, including VAT, is equal to 25% of the combined sums in paragraph (2)(a)(i) and (ii) which are ultimately recovered by the client.

(3) Subject to paragraph (4), in any other claim or proceedings to which this regulation applies, a damages-based agreement must not provide for a payment above an amount which, including VAT, is equal to 50% of the sums ultimately recovered by the client.

(4) The amounts prescribed in paragraphs (2)(b) and (3) shall only apply to claims or proceedings at first instance.

Information required to be given before an agreement is made in an employment matter
5.—(1) In an employment matter, the requirements prescribed for the purposes of section 58AA(4)(d) of the Act are to provide—
(a) information to the client in writing about the matters in paragraph (2); and
(b) such further explanation, advice or other information about any of those matters as the client may request.
(2) Those matters are—
(a) the circumstances in which the client may seek a review of costs and expenses of the representative and the procedure for doing so;
(b) the dispute resolution service provided by the Advisory, Conciliation and Arbitration Service (ACAS) in regard to actual and potential claims;
(c) whether other methods of pursuing the claim or financing the proceedings, including—
(i) advice under the Community Legal Service,
(ii) legal expenses insurance,
(iii) pro bono representation, or
(iv) trade union representation,
are available, and, if so, how they apply to the client and the claim or proceedings in question; and
(d) the point at which expenses become payable; and
(e) a reasonable estimate of the amount that is likely to be spent upon expenses, inclusive of VAT.

Additional causes of action in an employment matter

6. In an employment matter, any amendment to a damages-based agreement to cover additional causes of action must be in writing and signed by the client and the representative.

Payment in an employment matter
7. In an employment matter, a damages-based agreement must not provide for a payment above an amount which, including VAT, is equal to 35% of the sums ultimately recovered by the client in the claim or proceedings.

Terms and conditions of termination in an employment matter
8.—(1) In an employment matter, the additional requirements prescribed for the purposes of section 58AA(4)(c) of the Act are that the terms and conditions of a damages-based agreement must be in accordance with paragraphs (2), (3) and (4).
(2) If the agreement is terminated, the representatives may not charge the client more than the representative's costs and expenses for the work undertaken in respect of the client's claim or proceedings.
(3) The client may not terminate the agreement—
(a) after settlement has been agreed; or
(b) within seven days before the start of the tribunal hearing.
(4) The representative may not terminate the agreement and charge costs unless the client has behaved or is behaving unreasonably.
(5) Paragraphs (3) and (4) are without prejudice to any right of either party under general law of contract to terminate the agreement.

Signed by authority of the Lord Chancellor
Parliamentary Under Secretary of State
Ministry of Justice
Date

EXPLANATORY NOTE
(This note is not part of the Order)

These Regulations prescribe the requirements with which a damages-based agreement ("DBA") must comply in order to be enforceable under section 58AA of the Courts and Legal Services Act 1990 (c.41) ("the Act").

DBAs are a type of 'no win, no fee' agreement under which a representative (defined in these Regulations as a person providing the advocacy services, litigation services or claims management services to which the DBA relates) can recover an agreed percentage of a client's damages if the case is won ("the payment"), but will receive nothing if the case is lost.

Prior to amendment by the Legal Aid, Sentencing and Punishment of Offenders Act 2012 (c.10), section 58AA of the Act only provided for the regulation of DBAs used in employment matters. The effect of the amendment, subject to exceptions, is to permit and regulate the use of DBAs in all civil litigation.

These Regulations apply to all DBAs, including those which relate to employment matters, entered into or signed on or after the date on which they come into force. However, section 58AA(9) of the Act provides that, where section 57 of the Solicitors Act 1974 (c.47) applies to a DBA (other than one relating to an employment matter), it is not unenforceable only because it does not satisfy the conditions in section 58AA(4), under which these Regulations are made. Accordingly, article 1(4) excludes those DBAs to which section 57 of the Solicitors Act 1974 applies from the scope of these Regulations. Further, the effect of regulation 4 is limited to all DBAs other than those which relate to employment matters, whereas regulations 5, 6, 7 and 8 only apply to DBAs in respect of employment matters.

Regulation 2 revokes the Damages-Based Agreements Regulations 2010 (SI 2010/1206), which applied only to employment matters and which will continue to have effect in respect of any DBA relating to an employment matter signed before the date on which these Regulations come into force. However, these Regulations make similar separate provision in respect of employment matters.

Regulation 3 applies to all DBAs and specifies the requirements of a DBA.

Regulation 4, which applies to all DBAs other than those which relate to employment matters, provides that the payment from a client's damages shall be the sum agreed to be paid (which, where relevant, will include any disbursements incurred by the representative in respect of counsel's fees) net of any costs (including fixed costs), or sum in respect of counsel's fees, payable to the representative by another party to the proceedings.

Regulation 4 also provides that: in a claim for personal injuries, the amount to be paid by a client, including VAT, must not be greater than 25% of the combined total of the damages recovered by the client in the proceedings for pain, suffering and loss of amenity and pecuniary loss (other than future pecuniary loss), net of any sums recoverable by the Compensation Recovery Unit. The 25% cap will only apply to claims or proceedings at first instance; and in any other claim or proceedings to which these Regulations apply, the amount of the payment, including VAT, must not be greater than 50% of the sums ultimately recovered by the client. The 50% cap will only apply to claims or proceedings at first instance.

Regulations 5, 6, 7 and 8 apply only to DBAs in respect of employment matters.

Regulation 5 specifies the information that a representative must provide before a DBA is made.

Regulation 6 specifies that additional causes of action can be added to the agreement by written and signed amendment.

Regulation 7 provides for the maximum amount that is payable to the representative from a client's damages under a DBA in respect of an employment matter, so that the amount of the payment, including VAT, must not be greater than 35% of the sums ultimately recovered by the client in the claim or proceedings.

Regulation 8 states that the terms and conditions of an agreement that provide for the termination of the DBA in an employment matter must comply with the following requirements: if the agreement is ended then the representative cannot charge more than his or her costs and expenses for the work done in respect of the client's claim or proceedings; the client may not end the agreement at particular stages; the representative may not end the agreement unless the client has been or is being unreasonable; nothing in regulation 8 prevents a party from exercising a right under the general law of contract to terminate the agreement, for example for misrepresentation or fundamental breach.

Key Points:-

1. Claims may be better pursued under a hybrid DBA/CFA, following the new rules.

2. In a claim for personal injuries, the amount to be paid by a client, including VAT, must not be greater than 25% of the combined total of the damages recovered by the client in the proceedings for pain, suffering and loss of amenity and pecuniary loss (other than future pecuniary loss), net of any sums recoverable by the Compensation Recovery Unit. The 25% cap will only apply to claims or proceedings at first instance. It remains to be seen whether the government will change these rules.

3. The agreement must comply with Regulation 3 as above.

4. Any retainer must strictly comply with the 2013 DBA Regulations, or it will not be enforceable.

CHAPTER SEVEN
POTENTIAL ESCAPE ROUTES FROM FIXED COSTS

There is already a provision in the rules for an escape from fixed costs:-

45.29J Claims for an amount of costs exceeding fixed recoverable costs

(1) If it considers that there are exceptional circumstances making it appropriate to do so, the court will consider a claim for an amount of costs (excluding disbursements) which is greater than the fixed recoverable costs referred to in rules 45.29B to 45.29H.

(2) If the court considers such a claim to be appropriate, it may—
(a) summarily assess the costs; or
(b) make an order for the costs to be subject to detailed assessment.

(3) If the court does not consider the claim to be appropriate, it will make an order—
(a) if the claim is made by the claimant, for the fixed recoverable costs; or
(b) if the claim is made by the defendant, for a sum which has regard to, but which does not exceed the fixed recoverable costs,
and any permitted disbursements only.

45.29K Failure to achieve costs greater than fixed recoverable costs

(1) This rule applies where—
(a) costs are assessed in accordance with rule 45.29J(2); and
(b) the court assesses the costs (excluding any VAT) as being an amount which is in a sum less than 20% greater than the amount of the fixed recoverable costs.

(2) The court will make an order for the party who made the claim to be paid the lesser of—

(a) the fixed recoverable costs; and
(b) the assessed costs.

The Jackson report (July 2017) said this about the same provisions:-

5.20 Escape clause. CPR rule 45.29J enables a party to escape from the fast track FRC regime in exceptional circumstances. That provision will continue to apply, but its reach will be extended following the extension of FRC across the whole of the fast track. Use of this provision will continue to be rare, because any case of exceptional complexity is unlikely to be in the fast track.

The PI lawyers response provided:- *(vii) In any FRC regime there must be clarity about escape provisions.* It would seem that in reality the provision of any escape clause is unlikely to be allowed to any extent in the fast track. *In Parsa HHJ Tindal referred to the case of Costin v Merron [2013] 3 Costs LR 391 where Leveson LJ commented that 'exceptional' within the context of CPR 45.12 meant having spent exceptionally more money than would otherwise be the case. Whilst this may arise in the circumstances referred to by HHJ Wood and HHJ Walden-Smith, I have not heard any evidence on this point, and nor would I expect exceptional sums to be incurred within such a relatively short time period. On this definition of 'exceptional' I find that the Claimant has not surmounted the hurdle – cited in* ***KATHLEEN WHALLEY v ADVANTAGE INSURANCE CO LTD (2017)***

Important Fixed Costs Cases

In **TERRANCE BIRD v ACORN GROUP LTD (2016)**, the Court of Appeal found a disposal hearing was a "trial" where a personal injury claim had started under the Pre-Action Protocol for Low Value Personal Injury (Employers Liability and Public Liability) Claims and had settled after judgment but before trial. The Court said:-

"In my judgment listing a case for a disposal hearing following judgment, pursuant to Part 26PD12, is listing for trial, for the purposes

of triggering column 3 in Table 6D part B where a case which originated in the EL/PL Protocol settles after listing. My reasons follow.

First, listing a case for "disposal" means exactly what it says. The purpose of doing so is, so far as possible, finally to dispose of the case at first instance. A default or other judgment for damages to be assessed leaves that assessment outstanding, as the last stage in the final disposal of the proceedings. For that purpose it matters not whether the judgment has been obtained by default (as here) or on an application for summary judgment on liability, judgment on admissions, or after a liability only trial: see generally Part 26PD12(2).

The fact that it may be impossible to tell, prior to the disposal hearing itself, whether it will prove to be final in that sense, or merely the occasion for giving of directions, cannot be conclusive against listing of a disposal hearing triggering column 3 of Table 6D part B, because that table is concerned with settlement prior to trial. If the possibility of a disposal hearing being used for the giving only of directions were to be admitted, then it is hard to see how listing could ever be a trigger for the application of column 3 following a settlement. Even the hearing date of a full trial may turn into a hearing for directions if it proves impossible or unjust to do otherwise than permit an adjournment.

Secondly, the fact that a disposal hearing might prove to be uncontested is, again, neither here nor there. It is common ground that, even after a judgment in default, the defendant may attend and oppose the claimant's case as to quantification of damages at the disposal hearing. Again, if the possibility that such a hearing might prove to be uncontested were sufficient to prevent its listing being a trigger for the application of column 3, then that possibility exists at all kinds of final hearing, including traditional trials.

Thirdly, and as DJ Campbell emphasised, listing for a disposal hearing is the trigger for the claimant (and any other party which wishes to take an active part at that hearing) to prepare and serve the requisite evidence. Addressing the submission that there could be no move to column 3 if there had not previously been allocation to trigger column 2, she said, at paragraph 29 of her judgment:

"I am supported in this view by Mr Latham's submission that much work is to be done in cases which are heading to a disposal hearing, including the gathering of witness evidence, the preparation and service of written evidence which is specifically required by Practice Direction 26. 12.4(5). Indeed, there are a large number of cases which settle just before the disposal hearing or on the morning of it and I can take judicial notice of that fact as a judge who regularly deals with disposal lists. It cannot be right that those cases attract the same amount of costs as a case that settles after issue but before any allocation by the court which, if I were to accept the defendant's submissions, all those cases which will be months down the line from the listing of the disposal will only attract the costs in column one."

This court is entitled to give weight to these observations from a judge with large experience in this particular field. Furthermore, the appellant gains nothing from the fact that this particular disposal hearing was listed for a 10 minute hearing. The County Court at Birkenhead deals with the quantification of damages in relatively small claims of this kind within ten or fifteen minutes on a regular basis, even if opposed, with counsel on both sides. The cases are routinely disposed of on the papers, without oral evidence, after full pre-reading by the judge, and with the benefit of the most succinct submissions, in every respect proportional to the modest amounts usually at stake.

Fourthly, there is a useful pre-history to the formulation "final contested hearing" in Part 45.29E(4)(c). Part 45.15 deals with the success fee percentages applicable in road traffic accident claims. By Part 45.15(6)(b), as it was before April 2013, a reference to "trial" was a reference to the final contested hearing. This rule was introduced in 2004. Lamont v Burton [2007] 1WLR 2814 was about a road traffic accident claim which had concluded at a disposal hearing. It was taken for granted in this court (rather than determined after argument) that the disposal hearing had been a trial for the purposes of Part 45.15. I consider it very likely that, when it adopted the same definition of trial in 2013, for the purposes of fixed costs in EL/PL Protocol cases, the Rule Committee had the analysis in Lamont v Burton well in mind".

KATHLEEN WHALLEY v ADVANTAGE INSURANCE CO LTD (2017) – A claimant could not seek assessed costs, either on the standard or indemnity basis, in respect of the period of late acceptance. The entire claim fell within the fixed costs regime in CPR 45.29B. The Court said:-

75. ***I agree with Mr Arora's analysis. It is accepted that Part 36 is a self-contained code, as it could be argued is Schedule IIIA Part 45.29A et seq. This action was proceeding under the RTA Protocol and the only costs allowed are the fixed costs in CPR 45.29C and disbursements in accordance with CPR 45.29I (CPR 45.29B).***

76. *The Claimant's offer was by way of a Part 36 offer. Part 36 being a self-contained code also provides for the cost consequences from either the acceptance of an offer or either Party obtaining a more advantageous judgment at trial. Whilst Part 36 does contain specific exclusions in respect of the fixed costs regime, there is no specific exclusion in respect of this situation. This is in stark contrast to where a claimant accepts a defendant's offer either before or after the relevant time limit. As referred to above, where Part 36 modifies a general rule as to costs, Part 36 takes precedent. This was the situation argued in Broadhurst where there was perceived tension between CPR 36.17 and CPR 45.29B. However, Broadhurst was not determined by reference to Solomon.*

78. *In Broadhurst the Part 36 issue was wholly self-contained. However, Part 36 is silent as to the cost consequences on this scenario. Whilst the case law highlights this silence/omission, HHJ Walden-Smith and HHJ Gosnell refer to the omission as being deliberate to enable the court to exercise a board discre-*

tion, whereas HHJ Wood whilst also finding it was deliberate does so on the basis that the fixed costs rules prevail.

79. *I accept the reasoning of HHJ Wood that the 'omission' in addressing this specific situation was deliberate as costs, save for those specific situations excluded within Part 36, continue to fall for determination under CPR 45.29B. Whilst CPR 36.13(4) provides a mechanism for addressing the issue of cost, it is silent as to whether costs should be standard, indemnity or fixed. A failure to address a specific issue cannot be said to in some way modify the cost consequences of Part 45.*

80. *Alternatively, as per Solomon if there is a tension between CPR 36.13(4) and CPR 45.29B, I find that Part 36 is the general rule and Part 45 the specific rule. Part 36, in this particular case does not direct the court as to the specific consequences of accepting an offer where CPR 36.13(4) applies. The rule directs the court to determine the appropriate order for costs, albeit with a steer in favour of the claimant unless it is considered unjust. Further, CPR 36.13(4) does not direct that the court should allow costs on a standard, indemnity or fixed basis. CPR 36.13(3) is of no assistance as it does not apply to CPR 36.13(4). It follows therefore that CPR 36.13 is a general rule to apply to any situation. However, this is a 'fixed cost' claim and the specific rule as to costs is CPR 45.29B. If, there is tension, the specific gives way to the general. It is however not necessarily the case that there is a tension between CPR in my view, CPR 36.13(5) by being silent as to the basis of costs arguably does not contradict CPR 45.29B. 'Silence' does not equate to 'tension'"*

CHAPTER EIGHT
COUNSEL'S FEE AND DISBURSEMENTS IN THE NEW SYSTEM FROM OCTOBER 2018

Counsel's fees are also proposed to be amended by the Jackson report as follows:-

5.2 Ring fencing fees for counsel. Many practitioners, both solicitors and barristers, have urged the importance of ring fencing fees for counsel. The involvement of counsel at an early stage, both in advising and drafting, brings substantial benefits. ***Independent counsel bringing a fresh eye to the case can focus the litigation and sometimes bring about settlement. On the other hand, the rules cannot insist upon the use of counsel. Many other specialist lawyers bring the same benefits. In my view, for the reasons set out in chapter 5, the best course is to specify fees for items of work which are to be done by counsel or specialist lawyers.***

5.8 Counsel's fees. Many of the written submissions and many speakers at the seminars maintain that fees should be specifically ring fenced for counsel. They put forward two arguments with equal vigour:

(i) Ring fencing is necessary for the protection of the junior Bar, which is very much in the public interest.
(ii) Counsel's specialist input at an early stage is beneficial for the client and for the efficient conduct of the litigation.

Professor Richard Disney (one of my 14 assessors) has, with good reason, questioned the validity of the first argument. I do not see how I can recommend any reform because it is necessary to 'protect' one part of a profession. The professions exist to serve the public, not vice versa. It must be for the professions to organise themselves in whatever way is necessary to protect younger practitioners. The second argu-

ment, however, does have force in relation to the more complex fast track cases.

5.9 ***Does that mean ring fencing for barristers alone? No. Very often barristers will do the ring-fenced work and receive the ring-fenced fee. But on occasions the proper person to do the work and receive the ring-fenced fee may be a solicitor, for example the intended trial advocate. On some occasions the proper person to do the ring-fenced work and receive the ring-fenced fee may be a fellow of the Chartered Institute of Legal Executives with appropriate expertise. I shall use the phrase "counsel or specialist lawyer" to describe all such individuals.***

5.10 In relation to Bands 1, 2 and 3 (where there is currently very little ring fencing of fees for counsel) I recommend no change to the present rules, essentially for the reasons set out in chapter 15 of my Final Report. ***It is for solicitors to decide whether to do items of pre-trial work themselves or to instruct counsel. In relation to the new Band 4 and NIHL claims, however, I recommend a different approach.***

5.11 ***The mediated NIHL agreement provides that £500 be ring-fenced for settling the particulars of claim. I recommend that this should apply to all Band 4 cases.*** *The mediated NIHL agreement also provides that £1,280 be paid for restoring a company to the register. That includes both preparatory work and any necessary court appearance. This should apply in both NIHL and Band 4 cases. The mediated NIHL agreement recommends that other counsel fees should be recovered on top of the FRC, if justified. In my view that approach is too uncertain. I recommend that in NIHL and Band 4 cases separate fees should be recovered in respect of any of the following items done by counsel or specialist lawyers:*

Post-issue advice or conference £1,000 Settling defence or defence and counterclaim £500. Solicitors may well choose to instruct counsel or specialist lawyers in respect of other matters, but the

fees for that other work should not be recoverable as an addition to the monies set out in Tables 5.1 and 5.2.

5.12 Trial advocacy fee. The NIHL working group accepted that in NIHL cases the trial advocacy fees should be higher, but they could not agree on a figure. ***Having considered the rival arguments, I recommend the trial advocacy fee should be increased as follows for both Band 4 and NIHL cases:***

(a) Claim value up to £3,000 - Trial advocacy fee £1,380
(b) Claim value £3,001 to £10,000 - Trial advocacy fee £1,380
(c) Claim value £10,001 to £15,000 - Trial advocacy fee £1,800 Trial
(d) Claim value £15,001 to £25,000 - Trial advocacy fee £2,500

CPR rule 45.39, which provides some flexibility in respect of fast track trial costs will continue to apply.

Key Points:-

1. Counsel's fees shall NOT be ring fenced save in band 4 cases.

2. The Trial advocacy fee will be increased for band 4 claims.

3. Like current fast track fixed costs – the Solicitor will be liable for counsel's fees. Counsel's fees except in very narrow circumstances will not be recoverable as a separate disbursement.

Fixed Costs Disbursements

5.12 Disbursements. The above table does not include disbursements. The principal disbursements will be court fees, expert fees and (where ADR takes the form of mediation) the mediator's fee. In some cases, translators and/or interpreters are needed. I recommend that once the new fixed costs regime is in place, work should commence on developing fixed costs for experts. This is essentially what happened in the fast track. Once the fast track fixed costs for personal injury cases had been in place for a year, a scheme of fixed costs for medical reports22 was introduced: see chapter 15, paragraph 5.22 of my previous report and CPR rule 45.19. It would also be sensible to develop fixed costs for mediators, translators and interpreters.

CHAPTER NINE
CHANGES TO THE OPERATION OF PART 36 AND FIXED COSTS SUCCESS FEES

BROADHURST v TAN (2016), was an important case which set out the principle that in a fixed costs personal injury claim governed by CPR 45, costs were payable on the indemnity basis, where a claimant had made a Part 36 offer and then beaten this offer at Trial. The Court said in Broadhurst:-

8. A new rule 36.14A was also introduced to prescribe the costs consequences following judgment in section IIIA cases. While it modified some aspects of rule 36.14 (which set out the cost consequences following judgment) in fixed costs cases, it left rule 36.14(3) unmodified. Rule 36.14 provided, so far as material:

"36.14 – Costs consequences following judgment
(1)... (3)
Subject to rule 36.14A, this rule applies where upon judgment being entered...
(b) judgment against the defendant is at least as advantageous to the claimant as the proposals contained in a claimant's part 36 offer.

Subject to paragraph (6), where rule 36.14(1)(b) applies, the court will, unless it considers it unjust to do so, order that the claimant is entitled to –
(a) interest on the whole or part of any sum of money (excluding interest) awarded at a rate not exceeding 10% above base rate for some or all of the period starting with the date on which the relevant period expired;
(b) costs on the indemnity basis from the date on which the relevant period expired;
(c) interest on those costs at a rate not exceeding 10% above base rate and

(d) an additional amount, which shall not exceed £75,000, calculated by applying the prescribed percentage set out below..."

10. Rule 36.14A provided, so far as material:

"36.14A – Costs consequences following judgment where Section IIIA of Part 45 applies

(1) Where a claim no longer continues under the RTA or EL/PL Protocol pursuant to rule 45.29A(1), rule 36.14 applies with the following modifications.

(2) Subject to paragraphs (3),(3A) and (3B) where an order for costs is made pursuant to rule 36.14(2)-
(a) the claimant will be entitled to the fixed costs in Table 6B, 6C or 6D in section IIIA of Part 45 for the stage applicable at the date on which the relevant period expired; and
(b) the claimant will be liable for the defendant's costs from the date on which the relevant period expired to the date of the judgment.

(3) Subject to paragraphs (3A) and (3B) where the claimant fails to obtain a judgment more advantageous than the defendant's Protocol offer -
(a) the claimant will be entitled to the applicable Stage 1 and Stage 2 fixed costs in Table 6 or Table 6A in Section III of Part 45; and
(b) the claimant will be liable for the defendant's costs from the date on which the Protocol offer is deemed to be made to the date of judgment; and
...

(6) Fixed costs shall be calculated by reference to the amount which is awarded.

(7) Where the court makes an order for costs in favour of the defendant –
(a) *the court will have regard to; and*
(b) *the amount of costs ordered shall not exceed,*

the fixed costs in Table 6B, 6C or 6D in Section IIIA of Part 45 applicable at the date of judgment, less the fixed costs to which the claimant is entitled under paragraph (2) or (3).

(8) The parties are entitled to disbursements allowed in accordance with rule 45.29I incurred in any period for which costs are payable to them."

...

"I would allow the appeal in the case of Broadhurst and dismiss the appeal in the case of Smith largely for the reasons stated by Mr Williams.

If rule 45.29B stood alone, then subject to various rules in Part 45 which are immaterial, the only costs allowable in a section IIIA case to a claimant who was awarded costs following judgment in his favour would be "(a) the fixed costs in rule 45.29C and (b) disbursements in accordance with rule 45.29I". But rule 45.29B does not stand alone. The need to take account of Part 36 offers in section IIIA cases was recognised by the draftsman of the rules. Indeed, rule 36.14A is headed "costs consequences following judgment where section IIIA of Part 45 applies". Rule 45.29F (8) provides that, where a Part 36 offer is accepted in a section IIIA case, "rule 36.10A will apply instead of this rule". And rule 45.29F(9) provides that, where in such a case upon judgment being entered the claimant fails to obtain a judgment more advantageous than the claimant's Part 36 offer, "rule 36.14A will apply instead of this rule". Rule 45.29F does not, however, make provision as to what should happen where the claimant makes a successful Part 36 offer.

Mr Laughland submits that, since rule 45.29F makes no such provision, the basic or general rule in rule 45.29B that the only costs allowable are fixed costs and disbursements carries the day. But that is to ignore rule 36.14A which is headed "Costs consequences following judgment where section IIIA of Part 45 applies". Rule 36.14A(1) provides that in a section IIIA case "rule 36.14 applies with the following modifications". As we have seen, rule 36.14(3) provides that, where a claimant makes a successful Part 36 offer, the court will, unless it considers it unjust to do so, order that the claimant is entitled to four enhanced benefits including "(b) his costs on the indemnity basis from the date on which the relevant period expired".

The effect of rules 36.14 and 36.14A when read together is that, where a claimant makes a successful Part 36 offer, he is entitled to costs assessed on the indemnity basis. Thus, rule 36.14 is modified only to the extent stated by 36.14A. Since rule 36.14(3) has not been modified by rule 36.14A, it continues to have full force and effect. The tension between rule 45.29B and rule 36.14A must, therefore, be resolved in favour of rule 36.14A. I reach this conclusion as a straightforward matter of interpretation and without recourse to the canon of construction that, where there is a conflict between a specific provision and a general provision, the former takes precedence. As we have seen, there is disagreement as to which is the relevant general provision in the present context. Mr Williams submits that it is rule 36.14; and Mr Laughland submits that it is rule 45.29B. I do not find it necessary to resolve this difference.

Rule 36.14A(8) provides further support for my conclusion. This provision states that in a section IIIA case the parties (i.e. claimant as well as defendant) are entitled to disbursements allowed in accordance with rule 45.29I in any period for which costs are payable to them. This reflects rule 45.29B(b). If, as Mr Laughland contends, rule 45.29B prevailed over rule 36.14A in any event, this provision would have been unnecessary. It is significant that rule 36.14A does not contain a provision which reflects rule 45.29B(a) and 45.29C. In my view, the fact that rule 36.14A contains provision for payment of disbursements in accordance with rule 45.29B(b), but not for payment of fixed costs in accordance with rule 45.29B(a) confirms that the interpretation that I have adopted above is correct.

I find yet further support for the conclusion that I have reached in the wider contextual points made by Mr Williams to which I have referred at para 13 above which it is unnecessary to repeat.

For all these reasons, I do not consider that there is any doubt as to the true meaning of these rules. The tension is clearly resolved in favour of rule 36.14A. If that were wrong, then it would be legitimate to use the Explanatory Memorandum as an aid to construction (this was not the Explanatory Note to the statutory instrument). That is because the three conditions specified by Lord Browne-Wilkinson in Pepper v Hart [1993] AC 593 would be satisfied. First, the rules would, in material part, be obscure and/or ambiguous. Secondly, the Explanatory Memorandum was prepared by the Ministry of Justice (the promoter of the rules) and was laid before Parliament together with the 2013 Amendment Rules. I can see no difference in principle between a statement made in Parliament by a Minister or other promotor of a Bill and an explanatory memorandum laid before Parliament by the promotor of rules. The Rules are subject to the negative resolution procedure. Parliament has no power to amend the Rules, but could have annulled them if it had wished to do so. Thirdly, the statement in the Explanatory Memorandum relied on by the claimants is clear on the issue which arises on this appeal".

The Jackson report does propose change to the *Broadhurst* rules and says:-

Broadhurst v Tan and the effect of an order for indemnity costs. The one issue which cannot be ducked, however, is Broadhurst v Tan [2016] EWCA Civ 94; [2016] 1 WLR 1928. This decision, unless its effect is modified by rule change, will impact upon fixed costs generally. This issue is equally important in relation to higher value claims, but I deal with it here and will not repeat the discussion in later chapters. Views on this issue are sharply divided:

(i) Nine of my assessors consider that, although CPR Part 36 must continue to bring rewards for claimants who make effective Part 36 offers, in the context of a fixed costs regime it would be

better for there to be a percentage uplift on the fixed costs rather than an order for indemnity costs. *This will avoid the need for a detailed assessment of costs. Also, it will provide certainty for litigants. Certainty is an essential feature of an FRC regime. As to the level of percentage uplift, views range between 25% and 50%.*

(ii) Five of my assessors take the opposite view. Nicholas Bacon QC writes:

"I do not agree with the proposal that we do away with the Broadhurst indemnity costs order. These cases on indemnity costs are not clogging up the courts with detailed assessments. It is a powerful message for a party to consider rejection/acceptance. A 30% enhancement is not sufficient to redress the failure to accept an offer. It ignores the fact that as between solicitor and client more than the fixed costs will have been incurred by the client. Why should a client not be entitled to be reimbursed for their actual legal spend, rather than fixed costs, where a party has misconducted themselves or caused a party to incur costs unnecessarily because an earlier offer should have been accepted."

I have set out the competing arguments, because this is the only issue on which my assessors are sharply divided. After considering the powerful arguments on both sides, on balance, for the reasons set out in sub-paragraph (i) above, ***I favour replacing indemnity costs with a percentage uplift of 30% or perhaps 40%. BUT this is a clear issue of policy, which will need to be addressed in the consultation exercise following this report".***

CHAPTER TEN
DEVELOPING A PI PRACTICE IN THE NEW COSTS REGIME AND PREPARING FOR THE CHANGES

It is clear that these reforms are going to have a major impact on the personal injury and clinical negligence sector. I can draw the following conclusions from my work on this book:-

1. RTA personal injury firms will struggle in this new marketplace. We have already seen a number of such firms go out of business in late 2017 and early 2018. It is clear that CMCs will take over much of this work, and this does not seem to be opposed by current MOJ policy. If this work is to continue to be viable for Solicitors, changes to the 2013 DBA Regulations will be required to allow Solicitors to take more significant uplifts on these cases.

2. It may well be the case that with the new intermediate track, firms choose to employ more Counsel in house to work on these higher value cases and keep a larger percentage of the fees. Smaller firms will continue to use Counsel, as they currently do on fast track FRC cases. This has not changed a great deal since 2013.

3. It is likely there will continue to be a market for EL/PL and ELD claims. These cases (for the moment), escape the small claims track costs changes and the costs bandings are arguably workable to undertake this work.

4. There is a concern amongst some claimant lawyers that holiday sickness and travel claims, which are often heavily disputed and fought to Trial, are listed as a band 2 claim, when in fact, in reality it can be argued these cases (sometimes with experts on both sides), can be complex and difficult.

The changes had been proposed to come into effect for the small claims track and RTA changes (April or October 2018), but this is now realistically April or October 2019. Firms now have sufficient time to prepare and put these changes into effect.

'A Practical Guide to Dog Law for Owners and Others' by Andrea Pitt
'Ellis and Kevan on Credit Hire, 5th Edition' by Aidan Ellis & Tim Kevan
'RTA Allegations of Fraud in a Post-Jackson Era: The Handbook, 2nd Edition' by Andrew Mckie
'RTA Personal Injury Claims: A Practical Guide Post-Jackson' by Andrew Mckie
'On Experts: CPR35 for Lawyers and Experts' by David Boyle
'An Introduction to Personal Injury Law' by David Boyle
'A Practical Guide to Running Housing Disrepair and Cavity Wall Claims' by Andrew Mckie, Ian Skeate, Simon Redfearn
'A Practical Guide to Claims Arising From Accidents Abroad and Travel Claims' by Andrew Mckie & Ian Skeate
'A Practical Guide to Cosmetic Surgery Claims' by Dr Victoria Handley
'A Practical Guide to Chronic Pain Claims' by Pankaj Madan
'A Practical Guide to Claims Arising from Fatal Accidents' by James Patience
'A Practical Approach to Clinical Negligence Post-Jackson' by Geoffrey Simpson-Scott
'A Practical Guide to Personal Injury Trusts' by Alan Robinson
'Occupiers, Highways and Defective Premises Claims: A Practical Guide Post-Jackson' by Andrew Mckie
'Employers' Liability Claims: A Practical Guide Post-Jackson' by Andrew Mckie
'A Practical Guide to Subtle Brain Injury Claims' by Pankaj Madan
'The Law of Driverless Cars: An Introduction' by Alex Glassbrook
'A Practical Guide to Costs in Personal Injury Cases' by Matthew Hoe
'A Practical Guide to Alternative Dispute Resolution in Personal Injury Claims – Getting the Most Out of ADR Post-Jackson' by Peter Causton, Nichola Evans, James Arrowsmith
'A Practical Guide to Personal Injuries in Sport' by Adam Walker & Patricia Leonard

'A Practical Guide to Marketing for Lawyers' by Catherine Bailey & Jennet Ingram
'The No Nonsense Solicitors' Practice: A Guide To Running Your Firm' by Bettina Brueggemann
'Baby Steps: A Guide to Maternity Leave and Maternity Pay' by Leah Waller
'The Queen's Counsel Lawyer's Omnibus: 20 Years of Cartoons from the Times 1993-2013' by Alex Steuart Williams

www.ingramcontent.com/pod-product-compliance
Ingram Content Group UK Ltd.
Pitfield, Milton Keynes, MK11 3LW, UK
UKHW021239300926
15471UKWH00013B/763

9 781911 035596